Dear Ed,

I, the hope that we can solve our country's problems with wisdom and compassion.

Rob S

7/14/12

Published by
Caspian Publishing
Potomac, MD

Publisher's Cataloging-in-Publication Data
Sobhani, S. Rob.

    Press 2 for English : fix immigration, save America / by S. Rob Sobhani. – Potomac, MD : Caspian Pub., 2012.

    p. ; cm.

    Includes index.

    ISBN13: 978-0-9846538-0-5

    1. United States–Emigration and immigration–History–21st century. I. Title.

JV6456.S63 2012
304.873—dc22   2011941742

FIRST EDITION

Project coordination by Jenkins Group, Inc.
www.BookPublishing.com

Interior design by Brooke Camfield

Printed in the United States of America
16 15 14 13 12 • 5 4 3 2 1

Oh God, let this American democracy become glorious in spiritual degrees and render this just government victorious. Confirm this revered nation to upraise the standard of the oneness of humanity, to promulgate the Most Great Peace, to become thereby most glorious and praiseworthy among all the nations of the world. Oh God, this American nation is worthy of Thy favors and is deserving of Thy mercy.

—A prayer delivered in Chicago on April 30, 1912, by 'Abdu'l-Bahá, the son of the Prophet-founder of the Bahá'í faith—Bahá'u'lláh— who was visiting the United States at the behest of the nascent Bahá'í community in America. This prayer highlights America's critical role in the global community, and presents a moral mandate that we contribute to making the world a better place.

Contents

Preface

Land That I Love

I wrote this book because I love America. It is an exceptional place with exceptional people. It is a land where you can be anyone from anywhere and still make it—and I fear for America. I worry that America is losing its special character. I am convinced that if we do not address some of the problems we face, such as unemployment, the national debt, immigration, entitlement programs, and the erosion of our national fabric, we will leave a less prosperous and less cohesive nation to our children. This book focuses on one of these crises—immigration. Make no mistake about it: immigration is interconnected with every other critical issue.

Some people may argue that my stance is hypocritical since I am the son of immigrants. I was born in Ft. Leavenworth, Kansas, to Iranian parents. After the clerics took control of Iran in 1979, my parents fled their country. I have observed through their experiences the difficulties of cultural assimilation. But for me, there was never any ambivalence or question. I love America, and I am quite grateful that my parents came here.

So why would I, with my family background, be speaking out to challenge conventional wisdom on immigration? Why would I say that our immigration policies are leading to our decline? Some people might accuse me of trying to deny others the opportunity I had, but that is only half the story. If the theocratic dictatorship of the mullahs in Iran had not happened, millions of Iranians—including my parents—would never have been forced to leave their country. I am proud of my heritage. I named my son Cyrus because it reminds me and him that the first declaration of human rights was handed down by this benevolent leader after he freed the Jews from their Babylonian captivity. A son of Cyrus has been given a new lease on life in the land of Thomas Jefferson and George Washington. But life in the land the founders of America created is getting more difficult by the day.

Our country is economically broke. We do not have money to pay our obligations to our vulnerable citizens or to those who have fought our wars to keep us safe. We cannot afford to properly educate our children or build new roads and bridges. Yet we are still borrowing. We are also politically broke. Our exercise in harmonious democratic debate has come to an end. Both political parties have failed the American people. Every politician makes promises while knowing full well that he or she will not be able to fulfill them. A new reality in American politics has emerged; the delicate balance of democracy has shattered. Ours is a system in sclerosis.

Our failed immigration system is the flip side of a failed foreign policy. It is easier for our elected officials to pander to particular ethnic groups for votes than to point out the shortcomings of our neighbors. Mexican officials are allowed to export their revolution to the United States because not one single American president has insisted on good governance in Mexico. Meanwhile, our broken immigration system threatens the economic future of America.

Our country has grown from 200 million to more than 310 million in fewer than two decades. This means that our already-broken economic system needs to produce more jobs; protect more of the vulnerable; and build more schools, roads, and bridges. The problem is that the welfare system we have created along with a broken immigration system, is unaffordable under the demographic and economic circumstances of the twenty-first century.

Some would argue that we would not have become a global super-power without opening our doors to immigrants, that smart, self-motivated immigrants spur the innovations and create the jobs our economy needs to thrive. This may be true, but it does not tell the whole story. It is our system of government, our culture, our way of life that allowed Sonia Sotomayor to become the first Hispanic on the Supreme Court, Sergey Brin to cofound Google, Pierre Omidyar to found eBay, and Fareed Zakaria to rise to fame as a journalist and the host of a prominent TV show. There are hundreds of Sotomayors in Puerto Rico, , Brins in Russia, Omidyars in Iran and Zakarias in India. One of the main reasons why they are successful in America is because of our system. We need to export American values and know-how so the Sotomayors, Brins, Omidyars and Zakarias in Puerto Rico, Russia, Iran and India can find success at home.

I wrote this book as a wake-up call to America. Immigration, like Social Security, Medicare, Medicaid, and the Pentagon budget, has become the third rail of American politics. It is easier to demagogue than to solve the problem. Most of our public servants would rather get elected than address our problems with honesty and selflessness.

I chose to write about immigration because it is in many ways symptomatic of what ails America and because it is indeed connected to our other pressing issues such as job creation, reforming entitlements, bringing down our national debt, and rethinking our future infrastructure. Our roads and bridges are not Republican or Democratic; they are American.

The fundamental premise of this book is that we need to focus on good governance as the centerpiece of our foreign policy. We must insist not on democracy but on good governance because it affects us directly. If Mexico lacks good governance, it affects the United States. When the Iranian regime murders its citizens, stifles dissent, and forces its best and brightest to seek refuge in America, we need to call for a free and secular Iran. This would be good for America and good for the people of Iran. If our aid to the government of Pakistan finds its way into the pockets of corrupt officials, we have to cut off that aid. My heart aches for those hardworking people from El Salvador or Guatemala or Mexico or Iran who leave their countries in search of a better future for their families, but we cannot afford to allow other countries to export their problems of corruption, lack of good governance, and revolution to America. Instead, we must ask, What does it really mean to love our neighbors?

I am convinced that we can come up with a new immigration consensus that fixes the problem and in the process put America on the road to economic recovery. It will take strong leadership, but it can be accomplished. I realize that this is not a popular topic in many circles, but America is far too precious to keep silent.

For too long Washington has focused on our differences on immigration rather than on where we can agree. This has paralyzed the debate and invited demagogues to occupy center stage. The economics of immigration are clear: if we fix the system, we can create jobs for millions of Americans here and provide hope to millions who want to return to their native lands and help rebuild them.

The American eagle can soar again to new heights, but it cannot do so when its wings are heavy with the burden of masses of human beings flocking to our shores. However, this, too, can be fixed, for I believe that even though we may be broke, we are not broken. We may be in debt, but we are not paupers. We may be down, but we are not out. Our union may be on life support, but we are not dead. We are Americans, and our history of sacrifice, civility, innovation, and survival shows that we can meet any challenge, if only we have the will.

My love for America is deep, and it is this love that has inflamed my passion on immigration reform. I believe that without a single shot being fired, we are losing America. It's not like a war but rather like a cancer that is slowly growing and spreading, killing all that we hold dear. It must be eradicated, and I can think of no more important cause. I share the passion voiced in "Advice to My Country" by James Madison: "The advice nearest to my heart and deepest in my conviction is that the United States be cherished and perpetuated."

Acknowledgments

Writing this book has been a collaborative process. I could not have done it without the support and contributions of many people. First and foremost, I am grateful for the wonderful professionalism and guidance of my publisher, the Jenkins Group. In particular, the chairman and CEO, Jerry Jenkins, always gave me excellent advice every step of the way. Leah Nicholson, my editor, had superb instincts and patience throughout the process. Creative Director Yvonne Fetig Roehler made sure the book was designed beautifully. The people at Jenkins formed an effective team that always kept my best interests in mind. Leah also set me up with Catherine Whitney, a writer who worked closely with me to put my ideas into powerful prose. The final product is a tribute to a great team.

Over the years, I have been blessed with many strong colleagues, teachers, and friends. I am grateful to the late Georgetown University professor Jan Karski, who was the first to plant the idea of good governance in my mind. While I was a Ph.D. student at Georgetown University, others also allowed me to enhance my skills in understanding how nations interact. In particular I want to thank Robert Lieber, Eusebio Mujaleon, the late Avner Yaaniv, Madeleine Albright, and the late Jeane Kirkpatrick. Former Congresswoman Connie Morella, whom I worked for when she first ran for Congress, gave me my start at helping solve people's problems from the ground up.

Many immigration experts and scholars enlightened my work. I am especially thankful for the ideas and writings of Roy Beck, Mark Krikorian, and others at the Center for Immigration Studies, as well as academics and writers such as Samuel Huntington, Octavio Paz, and Daniel Cosio Villegas.

I want to thank my Home Depot friends, Anna R., and many more legal and illegal immigrants like them who informed my ideas in a personal way. Their longing for justice and a better standard of living for themselves and their families continue to be an inspiration to me. I also appreciate the contribution of my step-daughters' Spanish-speaking friends who translated for me on numerous occasions and were exceptional sounding boards.

I will always be grateful to my late father, who taught me that you can reach God by helping other people. This call to duty has been coupled by my mother's continuous reminder of the words of Saadi, the famous Persian poet:

> *Human beings are members of a whole,*
> *In creation of one essence and soul.*
> *If one member is afflicted with pain,*
> *Other members uneasy will remain.*
> *If you've no sympathy for human pain,*
> *The name of human you cannot retain!*

I am grateful to my wife, Guilda, for encouraging the narrative of seeking justice for those fleeing their countries. Between us, we have four lovely children—Cyrus, Ashley, Roya, and Leila—and it is my hope that the America they inherit is one in which commonsense solutions to our myriad challenges are tackled with compassion and wisdom.

Introduction

A Visit to the Underground Economy

Nearly 11 million undocumented immigrants currently live within our borders. That's 11 million people living in the shadows whom we know next to nothing about.

—New York Representative Steve Israel

Like thousands of Americans, I headed over to my local Home Depot on a recent Saturday in September. But my purpose was a bit different from most of theirs. I was looking for information and understanding, not hardware. On the way, I swung by Domino's Pizza and ordered three large pies and then Dunkin' Donuts for a couple dozen donuts.

At Home Depot, I pulled over to a corner of the vast parking lot where a group of men was gathered in a perpetual state of waiting. These were the day laborers, ubiquitous in many American communities, made up of mostly illegal immigrants hoping to get a job for a few hours to do landscaping, cleaning, construction, restaurant work, or any number of under-the-table arrangements. Home Depot has become a primary pickup site for day laborers across America because it is a convenient location for small contractors and landscapers. In my community in Maryland, the laborers hail mostly from Central and South America.

Carrying my towering boxes of pizzas and donuts, I wandered over to where a small group of men was standing. They greeted me with big smiles and open curiosity as I set down my offerings and introduced myself. I explained to Oscar, an English-speaking member of the group, that I was doing research on immigration and would appreciate a few moments of the group's time. They were happy to oblige, and Oscar agreed to translate. He told me that he and his companions came from El Salvador and all had children back home to whom they were sending support money, as well as children attending public schools in Maryland, Virginia, and Washington, D.C. There was Pablo with two children, Oseal with five children, and Carlo with three children. Oscar had one child. All of the men had been in America for four or five years, and they sent what money they could back home.

"Tell them I want to know why you're here—why you gave up so much to come and live like this," I said to Oscar. The question elicited a flurry of excited responses. Without exception, the men said that corruption in their homeland made it impossible for them to earn a living wage. Even if they could scrape together the average wage of $4 a day, it would be stolen from them. There was no rule of law. One of the men pulled up his shirt and showed me the scars from bullet wounds. "It's our country, and we love it," Oscar said, touching his heart, "but we are sick of the corruption. If it was governed by decent people, we'd go back."

As we spoke, the men kept watchful eyes on the lot behind me, where they were hoping that small contractors or home owners would pull up and offer them cash for work. What kind of work did they do? A little bit of everything, usually hard manual labor such as roofing, painting, hauling, and digging. The average wage was $8–$10 an hour. On a good day, they might work eight hours; more common was three or four hours. On some days, no trucks came or too few jobs were available for the dozens of men who gathered in the parking lot each morning. Oscar said that he tried to send $200–$300 home to El Salvador every month.

"How do you live?" I asked. Oscar replied that he and three others shared a low-cost apartment that was more like a rooming house with a small refrigerator and hot plate. Oseal and Carlo lived with relatives, also in cramped conditions. Six days a week they took buses to Home Depot. I was struck by how sad the men looked, and they acknowledged that they all dreamed constantly of the day they would return to their homes and families—although I had the impression that that day was still a long time coming. "We all miss our families very much," Oscar said with emotion, "but we need to do what is best for our children; otherwise, what kind of fathers would we be?"

It was impossible to listen to their stories without feeling for them. They were clearly hardworking, family-oriented men, with very little in their lives beyond the desire to make things better for themselves and their children. Yet I also realized that standing in parking lots while waiting for day jobs was no way to live. It was not the American dream for them or a healthy thing for us. This was an unhappy status quo.

One other common denominator among these men was their lack of formal education (none had graduated high school) and their poor English-language skills. These two strikes worked against their hopes to eventually save enough money to return home.

My forays to Home Depot were inspired by a desire to understand the motivations of people who come to America. In this case, they were illegals, driven by desperation and despair over the state of their homelands. But their reasons for coming to America weren't really that different from those of the thousands of legal immigrants who arrive on our shores every day. You don't leave behind a life and family to settle in a foreign land if your home country is a good place to live. Perhaps the onus should be on countries such as Mexico and El Salvador to provide good governance so the citizenry drain would not be so great.

The sad thing is that even as immigrants flock to America for a better life, neither legals or illegals seem to feel an incentive to assimilate into this country. During my September Home Depot visit, I was particularly interested in the subject of national loyalty. I wanted to know whether these men were developing a sense of belonging and caring. "Next week is the anniversary of 9/11," I mentioned before I left. "Will that day be any different for you?" They shrugged and shook their heads. "It's not important," Oscar told me. "It's an American concern. Not for us." In other words: "We're just dropping by to earn money. We're not part of who you are." As Oscar pointed out to me, "Why should we become Americans? We can watch TV in Spanish, listen to the radio in Spanish, buy groceries at Spanish markets, and do everything we need, just like home."

While, unquestionably, many immigrants assimilate more fully, I knew that large numbers lived in the reality Oscar described. It disturbed me to see the lack of emotional investment in a country that clearly represented survival and potential for them. The traditional immigration story was powerful because there was such a joy and sense of blessedness in the eyes of those who traveled far to be here. But I saw none of that sentiment in these men's eyes. This was strictly a business proposition for them—and not a very good one at that. Yet, at the same time I wondered, how can we expect assimilation when our system consistently downplays loyalty and deemphasizes American values?

As I drove away, I thought to myself that the issue was not about these men being Hispanic. If they had been Pakistanis or Egyptians, it would be the same situation because those governments have also failed their citizens—similarly with Russia, where corruption is rampant and poverty is on the rise. The point is that my Home Depot friends were here not because of their culture or the color of their skin. They were here because there were failed states south of our border.

In the following pages, I will tell the truth about immigration as it is seldom heard. Beyond the polemic on both sides of the issue is a simple truth: immigration once made our country rich, but this is no longer the case. We can feel compassion for those such as Oscar and his compatriots, but we cannot afford the levels of immigration that historically made our country a welcoming home for millions. As I talked with the men at the Home Depot parking lot, I thought about one of the virtues of the American way—which is to extend a helping hand to others. I believe in the virtue of charity, but I no longer believe that we are really helping anyone—least of all ourselves—by allowing these practices to continue. The underground parking lot economy doesn't really solve Oscar's problems, and it hurts American workers and taxpayers alike.

Is there a solution for Oscar? I determined that the most important contribution I could make to the immigration struggle would be to devise practical, commonsense solutions. In this book, I am setting out to do just that.

PART ONE:

THE CHALLENGE OF IMMIGRATION

Chapter 1

A Tarnished Golden Door

Send these, the homeless, tempest-tost to me,
I lift my lamp beside the golden door!

—from the Emma Lazarus poem
engraved on Lady Liberty's tablet

Thttps is a storm brewing, generated by too many huddled masses reaching our shores. It is time for us to face some tough realities, even those that challenge our most deeply prized ideas about our freedom-loving, compassionate, open-armed nation.

Taking a clear-eyed, unsentimental view, I believe that immigration, as it stands today, does not serve our national interest. We can't cling to romantic notions and fail to see the truth before us. Our current system of immigration is no longer a net plus but, in fact, may be quietly weakening our nation from within. While we should continue to celebrate the rich history of immigration and all that it has contributed to making this land the greatest on earth, we also must start better managing our immigration system.

The Statue of Liberty, our proud symbol of benevolence and welcome, seems almost anachronistic in light of our current troubles. We don't want the world to send its tired and its poor to our shores. We can't afford it! The golden door has lost its glitter. Immigration, once a vital part of our nation's wealth-building effort, is now jeopardizing our status as an economic superpower. We must still keep the doors open, but we can't afford the same levels of immigration that historically made our country the land of opportunity for millions of newcomers. According to the U.S. Census Bureau, since 1990 America's population has increased by 59 million—not including illegal immigration. That's nearly comparable to the entire population of France! Our resources are being depleted, our environment is being decimated, and our cultural fabric is being shredded. We are no longer a melting pot but a mixed salad—and a wilting one at that. Not only is our current immigration policy economically unsupportable but also it is culturally undermining the national fabric. I would also add that it is morally bad for our nation, as it ignores the injustices being done to those who have to leave their loved ones behind because their own governments didn't take care of them. The end result: American identity is now muddled and fuzzy.

The Immigration Galaxy

A galaxy with all the related issues spinning out. These include: jobs, health care, education, the environment, crime, housing, entitlements, wealth creation, national security, infrastructure, etc.

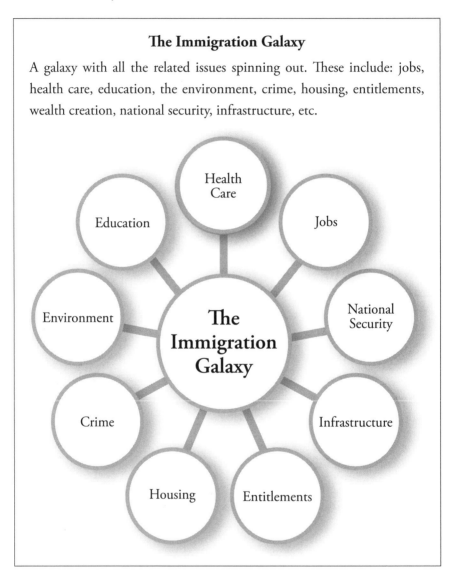

This plight is not just the result of the continued flow of illegals across our borders. Legal immigration is also taking a heavy toll. When the Statue of

Liberty was erected in 1886, with its poetic welcome to the peoples of the world, we were a nation in need of new blood. The huge surge of immigrants that came here during the late nineteenth and early twentieth centuries was considered a positive force. Nearly 25 million strong, they arrived from northwestern Europe, Italy, Greece, Russia, Hungary, Armenia, and Turkey. They traveled by boat and then continued by land across the vast, untapped American landscape. Advertisements lured them to come live in Kansas and Arizona and Oregon and Texas, to contribute their labors toward building a great melting pot of prosperity. America was the land of opportunity for them, but they were also essential to the national growth. It was a mutually beneficial arrangement that transformed this country into an economic, industrial, cultural, and political superpower. Keep in mind that these immigrants were not offered an *entitlement* but an *opportunity*.

Times have changed. Today, immigration, both legal and illegal, represents a drain on our nation's economic resources, a diminishment of our core identity, and a force for Balkanization, not unity. As an economist, I have studied the immigration problem from an economic perspective. As a citizen and the son of immigrants, I have contemplated the cost of continuing as we are versus changing course. As a human being, I am mindful of a moral obligation to help solve this problem that is a plague upon our communities and our world.

Unfortunately, the loud, often irrational, rhetoric from both sides of the political spectrum has made it difficult to make sense of the immigration crisis, much less develop solutions. This book is a challenge to government, business, and all of the activist organizations that resist change. For once, let's tell it like it really is and then see what we can do about it.

I'll begin with the hard truths:

IMMIGRATION WORSENS THE UNEMPLOYMENT CRISIS.

As I write this, our nation is suffering a severe jobs crisis, with unemployment stuck at around 9 percent. Nearly 20 million Americans struggle every day to find employment. It seems downright crazy to *deliberately* bring people to the United States to fill jobs Americans desperately need, but that is exactly what our government is doing. In 2009, the United States gave one million green cards and 450,000 work permits to foreign workers. Assuming all these green card holders are employed, that's approximately 1.5 million jobs that were denied to native-born Americans, and it's expected to be about the same for 2010. These job losses tend to hit communities where it hurts, in unskilled and low-wage areas typically filled by the lower middle class and America's working poor. Furthermore, according to the Pew Hispanic Center, when companies do begin hiring again, immigrants benefit from new jobs by a two-to-one margin.

The argument is often made that immigrants do only the jobs Americans won't do, but that is blatantly false and an insult to the American people. Americans are not lazy. An analysis of all 465 occupations defined by the Department of Commerce shows that even before the current recession, only four occupations were majority immigrant, accounting for less than 1 percent of the workforce. The basic law of supply and demand makes it very clear that our unemployment is directly linked to an oversupply of labor, much of it coming from legal and illegal immigrants. In short, the economy will benefit if we shrink the supply of labor from across our southern border that puts downward pressure on wages and unfortunately replaces native-born citizens, especially those within the black community.

According to the Bureau of Labor Statistics, workers without college degrees find well-paying jobs scarce. For those without high school diplomas, the situation is even more dire. The 25.3 million Americans over the age of 25 who do not have high-school diplomas now find themselves competing with immigrants from the Third World (both legal and illegal), who are generally less educated and relatively poor. Only 9.8 million of these undereducated Americans were working as of June 2011.

IMMIGRATION FLOODS THE UNITED STATES
WITH LOW-SKILLED LABOR.

The ideal immigration system is value added, which is how it is practiced in Canada and many other Western countries. Value-added means, with the exception of asylum seekers, immigrants should bring skills, education, and investment money to the table. They should, in effect, barter for the opportunity to live in America. Sadly, this is just a pipe dream. Our immigration policies favor what is euphemistically called "low-capital endowments"— unskilled, uneducated people who contribute little economically and instead drain state and local resources. According to a Center for Immigration Studies report, 42 percent of legal immigrants did not have high school educations, and 25 percent had less than a ninth-grade education. By maintaining this status quo, we are devaluing our own country and worsening our economy.

IMMIGRATION PUNISHES THE BLACK COMMUNITY.

Repeated studies have shown that mass immigration of unskilled workers has a particularly devastating effect on our nation's blacks— citizens who have struggled hard for equality and dignity. Studies prove that 40 percent of the decline in black employment is due to immigration. Unemployment is at a high of 17 percent in the black community, and in some communities it is much higher. The numbers among black teenagers are staggering: in 2010, the average unemployment for teenagers ages 16–19 was 45.4 percent among young men and 40 percent among young women. While blacks struggle to find a job, the restaurant industry in America—which attracts many low-skilled immigrants—has been one of the bright spots for hiring. More than 9.3 million people work in this sector, and job growth has been 2.1 percent from 2010 to 2011. For example, McDonald's hired 62,000 people on a national hiring day in April 2011. This job growth is expected to continue by adding 1.3 million jobs in the next decade. How many of the current 9.3 million and future 1.3 million will be filled by blacks is a question that must be answered by America's black leaders.

One would think that the Congressional Black Caucus and lobbying groups would take up this cause. Instead, they seem paralyzed in the face of reality and are unwilling to talk about the conflict within their constituencies. They have essentially sold out the black community.

The problem is worsened by the way affirmative-action policies treat all minorities equally. Any kind of minority status counts toward affirmative-action goals, so businesses regularly avoid hiring blacks in favor of immigrants. Under the banner of diversity, opportunities for blacks are cut off.

I understand that this is a tricky topic, since it is usually posed as a brown-versus-black conflict. Underlying racial tensions are difficult to address openly, but it is wrong to sacrifice the prospects of the black population, already struggling to untether itself from centuries of slavery and discrimination, to an open door policy. Immigration reform must address the correlation between black unemployment and immigration.

IMMIGRATION CREATES A NEW ENTITLEMENT CULTURE.

The principal menace facing America in the age of immigration is that needy immigrants will overwhelm our resources at the national, state, and local levels. The annual cost of illegal immigration is estimated at around $113 billion, which amounts to about $1,117 per legal household. I've heard the argument that even illegals pay taxes, and this is true, but FAIR notes that those receipts don't even come close to equaling the expenditures. On the state and local levels, where most of the cost is incurred, less than 5 percent of the outlay is recouped.

Legal immigration is also a burden on state and local governments. The basis of our immigration policy is "family reunification." When one member of an immigrant family gains a foothold, he or she begins a chain of migration by bringing the entire extended family. This places an enormous burden on our nation's resources. Consider just the oldest and youngest members of these families. Nearly two million legal immigrants are age 65 and older, utilizing the Medicare system. On the other end of the spectrum, the demands on public schools are staggering as a result of explosive growth in the population of new immigrant children. These demands include a growing bilingual education bureaucracy. The problem is exacerbated by so-called anchor babies—infants born to illegal residents who become instant citizens with a whole basket of benefits wrapped in a bow. There are around 350,000 such babies born each year, with an estimated annual price tag of $1.7 billion.

In short, the intersection of our entitlement programs with uncontrolled immigration can seriously impact our ability to maintain America's stellar credit rating. According to the *Wall Street Journal*, some 50.5 million Americans are on Medicaid, 46.5 million on Medicare, 52 million on Social Security, five million on SSI, and 44.6 million on food stamps and other nutrition programs. Some 24 million get the earned income tax credit, a cash income supplement. By 2010 such payments were 66 percent of the federal budget, up from 28 percent in 1965. We now spend $2.1 trillion a year on these redistribution programs.

Immigration has a significant environmental impact.

Today, immigration accounts for 90 percent of America's annual population growth. It is estimated that if immigration continues at the current rate, the United States will have 500 million people by 2050, nearly doubling our population. At a time when America is broke, we will have created an enormous burden on our transportation infrastructure and water resources. Our once-vast landscape will be squeezed and stressed to the breaking point.

It's just common sense that a population explosion will have a brutal effect on the environment—especially when you consider that developed countries such as the United States have 32 times the environmental impact of developing countries. Scientists estimate that average U.S. immigrants produce about four times more CO_2 here than they would in their countries of origin. That's because when they come here, they do not maintain the simpler lifestyles of their home countries. The carbon footprint of immigrants is large and growing. The "consumption effect" alone is huge. Once in America, it's a steady track to consumer behavior that involves cars, new housing, technology, and regular flights back home. The net effect is less green. But the real danger is in overpopulation itself. If growth continues at its current rate, it will strip our nation of valuable natural resources and create a toxic environment within the next 50 years.

IMMIGRATION FRACTURES OUR
PRECIOUS NATIONAL IDENTITY.

Not only are we allowing 1.5 million new residents a year and tolerating the presence of millions of illegals but also we are making little effort to culturally assimilate them. The title of this book, *Press 2 for English*, was born of this disturbing new reality: immigrants want to be here, but they have very little incentive to assimilate and become part of the American fabric of shared values—history, culture, and language. The open-border advocates tell them that we are a multicultural nation of immigrants (a mixed salad) rather than a unified nation composed of people from many countries (a melting pot). Separation, not assimilation, has become the norm. If you are Spanish speaking, you can conduct all your business in your native tongue—the Department of Motor Vehicles, schools, courts, airports, unemployment offices, and voting ballots are all set up to make things comfortable for non-English speakers. You can even take a citizenship test in Spanish. What a country! We do not even insist that our native tongue be the national language. It is the height of irony to watch swearing-in ceremonies for new citizens conducted in their native languages rather than in English.

The previous waves of immigrants who built America were highly patriotic. They were proud to be Americans, and they happily assimilated into the culture, including embracing the English language. This is no longer true. We have lost sight of how much common aspirations and practices matter to the strength of a nation.

IMMIGRATION RETARDS STABILITY
IN THIRD WORLD COUNTRIES.

If we care about global stability—and we must—it should be clear that U.S. immigration policies are not doing the people of the world any favors. Those who preach an open-door policy out of a sense of compassion toward those in need should understand that when citizens desert a poorly run and economically unstable country, it becomes further destabilized. If there is no incentive to stay and build, the citizens will disperse and these nations will eventually collapse in on themselves.

We are already witnessing examples of this. It's just a fact that most illegals flooding our borders are Mexican, but also one-third of legal immigrants are from Mexico. One might ask, Why do so many people from Mexico want to come here? According to Foreign Affairs, in the last decade between 90–98 percent of the Mexican nationals who tried to enter the U.S. illegally were ultimately successful. What is wrong with their country? Conditions in Mexico are rife with corruption and violence. Ordinary people cannot make close to a living wage. The Mexican government, instead of taking steps to resurrect its economy and political structure, seems to favor the idea of "exporting" its poorest and most vulnerable citizens to America while maintaining its corrupt status quo. Former Mexican dictator Porfirio Diaz was once quoted as saying: "Poor Mexico! So far from heaven, so close to the United States." Although we are neighbors, we tolerate this situation instead of pressuring Mexico to become a nation of laws.

Contrast that with Costa Rica. Costa Rica does not export its poor to the United States because its political culture emphasizes the rule of law and a commitment to developing socioeconomic prosperity for its people. In fact, when Costa Rica declared its independence from Spain in 1823, the cornerstone of its democracy became education: "The provision of education is the essential foundation of individual happiness and the prosperity for all." Today, 35 percent of Costa Rica's budget is devoted to education. Equally important, Costa Rica's national culture is a social activity in which the preservation, development and recognition of the country's achievements are emphasized. The relationship between literacy and political culture in Costa Rica has led to electoral democracy, civic peace and an economy that exports goods not humans. This is in sharp contrast to its neighbors.

In an essay called "Mexico's Crisis," its greatest intellectual Daniel Cosio Villegas describes his country's problem as the lack of "educative action to give Mexicans a common consciousness of their interests and their problems." And Octavio Paz, Mexico's Nobel Laureate, lays the blame on his country's socio-political culture: "In a world of violence and suspicion, ideas and accomplishments count for little. The only thing of value is manliness, personal strength, and a capacity to impose oneself on others."

The United States is a major force in the world and spends billions to help stabilize third world countries, but we have failed to make the connection that our open-door policies actually contribute to declining standards of living in troubled societies.

An example very close to my heart is the Iranian diaspora. Since the Islamic Revolution of the 1970s and during the ensuing economic deterioration in recent years, Iran's "brain drain" has steadily worsened. Brain drain is measured by the number of people with higher education that emigrate from a country. A 2006 study by the International Monetary Fund ranked Iran first in brain drain among 90 countries. High unemployment, economic insecurity, political unrest, religious fundamentalism, and censorship all contribute to the desire of Iran's educated classes—especially young people and those with advanced degrees in science and technology—to leave their country behind. The race to emigrate shows no signs of abating. It is estimated that more than 150,000 new college graduates leave Iran every year.

While we might initially welcome these high-quality immigrants from Iran in America, the consequences of a failed Iran will have global implications. The problems that plague Iran and other nations cannot be solved by a diaspora of the best and brightest citizens. Instead, the United States and like-minded nations should provide moral, financial, and diplomatic support to the people of Iran to change the clerical regime and restore the intellectual and economic vitality that once made Iran a center of prosperity. Iran—like Mexico, China and Russia—is full of talented, hard-working, freedom-loving people. It is in America's interest to keep the door open for the millions of Iranians who want to visit, but it is even more important to support a transition from theocracy to democracy for those who want to rebuild in Iran.

It's time for a change, and the majority of Americans agree. In a survey conducted by the Polling Company during the 2010 midterm elections, 61 percent of voters believed that President Obama had not been aggressive enough in enforcing federal immigration laws. Sixty-nine percent of respondents also said that they consider immigration to be an important public policy issue. A measly 4 percent of respondents believed the president had been too tough in enforcing immigration laws. The midterm voters also expressed strong support for the principle that states should play a major role in enforcing immigration laws. Fifty-three percent favored an Arizona-style law passed in their own state.

These results show an important trend in public attitudes. While immigration was not the central issue during the 2010 elections, the results of the elections produced a shift in the immigration balance of power, with the defeat of more than 40 open-border incumbents in the House of Representatives. These representatives were replaced by those who supported tougher immigration enforcement and opposed amnesty for illegal aliens.

This great American experiment is still relatively young, but we have reached a turning point. Will we go forward strong and unified, or will we allow our nation to become fragmented and diminished? The choice is ours.

Chapter 2

The Cost of Immigration

*Posterity: you will never know how much it
has cost my generation to preserve your freedom.
I hope you will make good use of it.*

—John Quincy Adams

One would have to be made of stone not to feel compassion for the desperate immigrants who leave behind their families and risk everything to make a better life in America. Americans are compassionate people, and our heartstrings are easily tugged by these stories. We are proud to serve as a lifeboat to so many poor and disenfranchised souls.

But think about a lifeboat for a moment. By its nature, a lifeboat has a set circumference and will hold only a limited number of people. If it's a real emergency, maybe you can squeeze a few more in—but not many. If the boat becomes overloaded, it will tip over or sink, which would make it a *death* boat. The fortunate people who have found seats in the lifeboat can look with compassion on those who are trying to squeeze in and overload the boat. But they can also understand that to act on their emotions could doom them all.

I find myself feeling this way when I speak to immigrants and hear their stories, especially those from Mexico and Latin America, who are hardworking, God-fearing people. It is hard to resist embracing them and saying, "We must find a place for you here." But, intellectually, I know that is not the answer. America cannot become that sinking lifeboat.

A more colorful way of making this reality check is Roy Beck's "immigration gumball theory," which recently went viral on YouTube when a speech he gave was viewed by millions of people. Beck, an innocuous middle-aged policy wonk, is not at all the type one would think of as a YouTube star. He has long been an immigration expert, and as the executive director of NumbersUSA, he daily challenges our nation's open-border policies. In his viral video, Beck stands on a stage with a prop, a giant jar stuffed with hundreds of gumballs. The gumballs, he explains, represent 4.6 billion people in the world who live in impoverished conditions. Grabbing a small handful of gumballs from the top of the jar, he says, "These represent the one million people our immigration policy rescues from third world poverty every year." On the video, the murmurs of amazement from the audience grow loud as it becomes glaringly obvious that this number represents only a tiny fraction of the total gumballs. Holding up his giant jar of poverty, Beck announces, "If we care about people, we have to find ways to help them *there*." Translated into policy, this means we will have to focus on good governance in Mexico and Latin America. We must insist on justice for Mexicans *in* Mexico.

The failure of our compassionate immigration policy is plain for all to see in Beck's gumball jar. We cannot "save" 4.6 billion people by bringing them to our shores; we can't even make a dent in the problem of global poverty.

Here's the bottom line: when we cut through all of the arguments and emotion, we find not only that we cannot save the world through immigration but also that we can no longer afford to try. It's a lose-lose situation. This is a cold, hard reality, a matter of dollars and cents. I'm speaking not only of illegal immigrants but also of *all* immigrants. We must do a better job of managing immigration.

When people talk about the problem with immigration, they are usually referring to illegals. It's so easy to scapegoat the rule breakers and those like my Home Depot friends. But the truth is that the 11 or 12 million illegals in this country represent only a fraction of the problem. Immigration itself is a broken system that has become both financially and culturally unsustainable.

A recent article in the *National Review* was cleverly titled "Legal, Good/ Illegal, Bad? Let's Call the Whole Thing Off." Author Mark Krikorian, director of the Center for Immigration Studies, wrote that most Americans—many of whom were raised on romantic stories told by grandparents and great-grandparents who immigrated here—are captivated by the fallacy that if we solve the illegal problem, we'll be on solid ground. But it's a brutal fact that both legal immigration and illegal immigration represent a drain on our resources, a diminishment of our central identity, and a force for fragmentation, not unity. In a 2006 report by the Brookings Institution that named the greatest public policy failures since World War II, immigration ranked number 2.

Don't get me wrong. America is still a great nation. It's great because of its values, its culture, and the Constitution. That's why it remains a magnet for those who are dissatisfied with their own countries. But we are in a period of extreme economic pressure, and that is why it is essential that we rethink our immigration policy.

In his article, Krikorian points out that the distinction between legal immigration and illegal immigration doesn't get us very far in the discussion, as "the legal and illegal immigration flows are inextricably intertwined. It's not as though legals are from Mars and illegals are from Venus—they come from the same countries, live in the same communities and families, and are often the same exact people . . . . It's not much of an exaggeration to say that our 'legal' immigration system is a permanent rolling amnesty for illegal aliens." What he means by this is that not every illegal swims through a muddy ditch or jumps a fence to be here. The more common means of passage is a temporary permit that is allowed to expire. Since we don't have the means or the will to track down and deport the malingerers, they remain here as illegals and eventually gain legal status.

Even so, people might still wonder why *legal* immigration is a problem. The argument we hear most often in favor of open borders is that, except for Native Americans, we are all immigrants. We all have ancestors who came here from somewhere else, and because our ancestors assimilated, others will, too. But to compare the profile of today's immigrants with one long ago is to remain blind to reality. When vast numbers of Europeans came to the United States during the great waves in the late nineteenth and early twentieth centuries, they departed by boat with the expectation of never seeing their homelands again. To survive in America, they knew that they had to embrace their new land, adopt its language and culture, and never look back. They learned English and worked hard to assimilate, and while they initially settled in dense ethnic communities, they soon spread out across America to follow opportunities. It was not uncommon for immigrants to Americanize the family name so as to fit in—an example being Ralph Lauren, whose birth name was Lifshitz.

Today's immigrants can easily bounce back and forth between their home countries and America. They come for economic opportunity, but assimilation is a choice, not a necessity. Hispanic immigrants, in particular, have little motivation to assimilate or learn English. According to the Pew Hispanic Center, only 52 percent of Hispanic naturalized citizens speak English well, in part because we have become a multilingual society where virtually all official business can be conducted in Spanish. Isolated in closed communities, they create mini-Mexicos and mini–Latin Americas in towns and cities where they live.

Generations of Exclusion, a book by Edward E. Telles and Vilma Ortiz, analyzed four generations of Mexican Americans from Los Angeles and San Antonio. The authors found that they were very slow to assimilate. Not until the fourth generation were inroads made on simple gestures such as socializing with non-Mexican friends. By the fourth generation, 20 percent were still below the poverty level, suggesting an ingrained culture of dependency. Most troubling, consistent with a decline in higher education in the third and fourth generations, was a rise in birthrates. According to the *Washington Post*, high birth rates, more than immigration, now account for the surging growth in population among Hispanics. From 2000 to 2010, 60 percent of the growth in Hispanic population came from births. For example, the population of Mexicans grew to 7.2 million during the last decade from births. In short, the size of the Hispanic population has doubled since 1990 to 50.5 million. This suggests that more than 80 percent of U.S. population growth through 2050 will come from Hispanic immigrants and their children.

Ronald G. Corwin, professor emeritus, Department of Sociology, Ohio State University, has conducted extensive studies about the economic impact of immigration. The picture he paints is bleak:

> *While the long-term economic consequences of immigration, and illegal immigration in particular, are still being debated, it seems clear that over the next few generations at least, the costs that illegal households impose on the society in the form of treatment for the uninsured, federal aid to schools, federal prisons/courts, and the immigration system will exceed by far the taxes they pay. The economic costs imposed by illegal immigrants are especially burdensome in California and some other border states that must assume the steep costs of educating their non-English speaking*

children. And, beyond these economic costs, immigration is having serious adverse affects on already unacceptable levels of social stratification. Competition for unskilled jobs with high school drop outs from Mexico has depressed the wages and increased the unemployment rates of black males, including especially youths and high school drop outs. Correspondingly, immigration has seriously compounded already unacceptably high levels of poverty and residential segregation, and it is largely responsible for segregated, overcrowded schools in many cities. Furthermore, other facets of the social structure are also being adversely affected, as many immigrants, especially those from Mexico, are imprisoned, participate in violent gangs, and perpetuate an illegal workforce and an underground economy that thrives on identity theft and human smuggling.

It is therefore not surprising to see headlines such as, "How Los Angeles Lost Its Mojo," by Joel Kotkin in 2011 arguing that "the city's misguided political leaders could turn this economic dynamo into an Athens by the Pacific." The political leaders he is referring to are labor unions and the political leadership of the Latino community.

People who point out these obvious problems are often called racist, especially by the well-organized open-border lobbies. This is a distraction from the true issue. It is not racist to speak the truth, and any statistical analysis backs up Professor Corwin's points. In my view, we have a choice: we can hide behind a false sense of political correctness that defends the indefensible, even as we watch this nation decline, or we can look at the facts objectively. Our immigration policies are contributing to the rise of a permanent underclass. A study by the Tomas Rivera Policy Institute at USC stated that, on average, a Latino immigrant will spend 20 years working just to achieve the same standard of living as a U.S.-born Latino. Immigrants account for one-fifth of the population living in poverty, and that number rises to one-half in California and one-third in New York, New Jersey, Florida, Texas, and Arizona.

For me, the most disturbing area of Professor Corwin's research is his review of immigration's impact on our educational standards and our status in the world. He points out that the United States became a superpower in the twentieth century in large part because we made a firm commitment to higher education—far more than any other developed nation. But this is no longer the case, and a big reason is that our school systems, especially in states such as California, Arizona, Texas, and Florida, are flooded with non-English-speaking children whose parents are uneducated and poor. The school systems cannot begin to accommodate them. Third world cultures have not traditionally had the same commitment to education, and if our schools are filled with students for whom education is not a priority, they can soon drag down the whole system. Indeed, America no longer ranks in the top tier in any measure of educational achievement.

One recent evening, I found myself chatting with a woman who taught English as a second language. Naturally, I was curious about her observations. She told me that the kids in her ESL class were mostly illegal, as were their parents, and many of the parents were illiterate. "Enormous funds are being allocated to teach these kids and create a support system," she said. "It is truly an entitlement encouraged by the teachers union. A whole lobby has developed in support of English as a second language." She admitted to feeling overwhelmed by the sheer numbers of students who required exceptional help. She wanted very much to provide that help, but she feared the task was too great.

The status of America as a superpower will depend on our being well educated. It is important to the world that the United States lead so the vacuum is not filled by less benevolent nations such as China and Russia. It is in the interest of the world that America lead the coalition of freedom-loving states, not the amoral governments of Russia and China. Allowing the Chinese or Russian governments to lead will mean no chance of freedom for those trapped in Zimbabwe, Iran, Libya or Syria.

Welfare Use by Immigrants

An April 2011 report by the Center for Immigration Studies, authored by Steven A. Camarota, sheds a disturbing light on immigrants' use of aid programs. Among the findings:

- In 2009 (based on data collected in 2010), 57 percent of households headed by an immigrant, legal and illegal, with children under 18 used at least one welfare program, compared with 39 percent for native households with children.
- Immigrant households' use of welfare tends to be much higher than that of natives for food assistance programs and Medicaid.
- Immigrant households with children used welfare programs at consistently higher rates than did natives, even before the current recession.
- 52 percent of legal immigrant households with children used at least one welfare program in 2009, compared with 71 percent for illegal immigrant households with children. Illegal immigrants generally receive benefits on behalf of their U.S.-born children.
- Illegal immigrant households with children primarily use food assistance and Medicaid and make almost no use of cash or housing assistance. In contrast, legal immigrant households tend to have relatively high rates of use for every type of program.
- High welfare use by immigrant-headed households with children is partly explained by the low education level of many immigrants. Of households headed by an immigrant who has not graduated high school, 80 percent access the welfare system, compared with 25 percent for those headed by an immigrant who has at least a bachelor's degree.
- An unwillingness to work is not the reason immigrant welfare use is high. The vast majority (95 percent) of immigrant households with

children had at least one worker in 2009. But their low education levels mean that more than half of these working-immigrant households with children still accessed the welfare system during 2009.

- Welfare use tends to be high for both new arrivals and established residents. In 2009, 60 percent of households with children headed by an immigrant who arrived in 2000 or later used at least one welfare program; for households headed by immigrants who arrived before 2000, it was 55 percent.

A SOBERING JOBS PICTURE

In September 2010, Camarota gave sobering testimony to the House Judiciary Committee Subcommittee on Immigration, Citizenship, Refugees, Border Security, and International Law. The topic of discussion was "New Jobs in Recession and Recovery: Who Are Getting Them and Who Are Not." Camarota's testimony focused solely on the economic costs of legal immigration. He pointed out that although immigration increases the overall size of the U.S. economy (more workers means a bigger gross domestic product), the vast majority of this increase goes to the immigrants themselves in the form of wages and other compensation. Camarota posed the question, How much, if at all, does the existing population benefit? He cited approximately 2.7 percent, or $375 billion in wage losses suffered by American workers because of immigration. This is the money that would have gone to workers as wages if there were no immigration.

Camarota's conclusion was that although immigration increases the economy, the actual benefits to native Americans are just not there. Immigration increases our population growth but slows our national economic growth because the greater population does not increase productivity. Because the labor pool is low skilled and poorly educated, it is often a drain on local, state, and federal budgets. In short, the new arrivals are not wealth creators but are, for the most part, a burden on the economy.

Myth vs. Reality: Native or Immigrant Worker?

These jobs are often cited as being filled by immigrants because Americans don't want to do them. In reality, they are majority-American jobs.

JOB	% NATIVE WORKERS	% IMMIGRANTS
Maids and housekeepers	55	45
Taxi drivers/chauffeurs	58	42
Butchers/meat processors	63	37
Construction laborers	65	35
Janitors	75	25

Source: *Center for Immigration Studie*

Also testifying was Dr. Rakesh Kochar, associate director for research at the Pew Hispanic Center. Dr. Kochar told the committee that the recovery might be leaving native-born Americans behind in favor of immigrants. The Pew study compared the job picture among native-born and immigrant Hispanics during a three-month period in the spring of 2010. Compared with the same period in 2009, this period showed that immigrant workers gained more than 650,000 jobs while native-born workers lost 1.2 million jobs. In particular, immigrant Hispanics gained 98,000 new jobs in construction while native-born Hispanics lost 133,000 jobs and native-born non-Hispanics lost 511,000 jobs. Hispanic immigrants gained 26,000 jobs in finance, real estate, and insurance while native-born Hispanics lost 18,000 jobs and native-born non-Hispanics lost 112,000 jobs.

Economist Heidi Shierholz, from the Economic Policy Institute, testified that despite the fact that economists have declared an official end to the recession, there are still 5.4 percent fewer jobs available than when the recession began in 2007. Noting that the immigration system is unresponsive to economic cycles, Shierholz said, "In 2010, the unemployment rate in construction was over 20 percent, but the Department of Labor nevertheless certified thousands of H-2B visas for construction workers. This defies logic." She argued that immigration reform should take into account the needs of the economy, especially the employment situation.

I am writing this book just as the United States is beginning to tiptoe out of the worst recession in our lifetimes. More than nine million jobs were swept away in a two-year period. Yet, in 2009, the United States gave one million green cards and 450,000 work permits to foreign workers. That's approximately 1.5 million jobs that were denied to native-born Americans, and it's expected to be about the same in 2010. These job losses tend to hit communities where it hurts, in unskilled and low-wage areas typically filled by the lower middle class and America's working poor.

"There is a substantial difference in how the economic recovery is working out for the native-born and the foreign-born," Dr. Kochhar told *The Washington Post.* "Only the immigrant experience has been a positive one."

As an early indicator of a larger trend, it is alarming. The Pew Report did not distinguish between legal immigrants and illegal immigrants, and it did not speculate about the reasons for the disparity. I can think of an obvious one: the cost of labor.

THE HIGH COST OF CHEAP LABOR

With a wink and a nod, there is a broad acceptance in the business community of the presence of up to 12 million illegals in the country. Simply put, that is a big reason why there seems to be little political will to do anything about the problem. Cheap labor is cheap labor, and it's even more appealing during tough economic times. Even so, we are a nation of laws, and the law on hiring illegal aliens is quite clear:

> *Anyone employing or contracting with an illegal alien without verifying his work authorization status is guilty of a misdemeanor. Aliens and employers violating immigration laws are subject*

to arrest, detention, and seizure of their vehicles or property. In addition, individuals or entities who engage in racketeering enterprises that commit (or conspire to commit) immigration-related felonies are subject to private civil suits for treble damages and injunctive relief.

It is quite possible that most of us have hired an illegal at one point, without necessarily knowing it—a landscaper, handyperson, housekeeper, or the like. Most analyses of illegal aliens conclude that employment is the single most important factor for an undocumented person taking the risk; if people did not employ illegals, they would not come here. So who are the culprits flaunting the law to take advantage of this cheap labor? WeHireAliens.com, a watchdog group committed to exposing companies that hire illegals, has outed nearly 6,000 companies representing all 50 states. In the site's Hall of Shame, there are hundreds of companies large and small, in virtually every field, from electronics to automotive to corporate services—in addition to the more traditional occupations of food services, housekeeping, and landscaping.

Ironically, these include the U.S. Forest Service, the Postal Service, and the city government of Houston. The site also sponsors a national boycott of some of our most iconic companies, including Miller Brewing Co., McDonald's, Bank of America, and State Farm Insurance.

Why do companies hire illegals? Well, first of all, because they *can*.

Enforcement has been notoriously lackluster for as long as anyone can remember. When high-profile corporate busts are made, they have little effect on the companies. For example, Wal-Mart was fined $11 million in 2005 for hiring contractors that used illegals; the sum was tantamount to a slap on the wrist. But such attempts to enforce the law on a large scale are few and far between. Business and government regularly collude in a "don't ask, don't tell" atmosphere, especially for middle-class Latinos who are part of communities with purchasing power.

In 2007, Arizona enacted a law containing what then-Governor Janet Napolitano (now head of the Department of Homeland Security) called the "business death penalty," a provision threatening companies that hired illegal aliens with revocation of their corporate charters. But that law is still slowly making its way through the courts, and years after the fact, few people believe it will ever be enacted—especially now that Arizona has passed new laws bypassing it. The reason the 2007 law bears mentioning, however, is that the U.S. Chamber of Commerce has been the primary challenger and still vows to take the matter all the way to the U.S. Supreme Court if necessary. The chamber's fear is that the law, if enacted, would spread elsewhere and crush businesses nationwide.

CHAMBER OF COMMERCE: ON THE WRONG SIDE

Does the Chamber of Commerce's anti-enforcement stand represent the attitudes of business? Are business and labor at odds on the issue of illegal immigrants? The common perception has been that workers want stricter enforcement because they're the ones with jobs at stake, while businesses want looser enforcement because it costs them more and prevents them from hiring cheap labor. However, a 2010 Zogby poll of senior executives, business owners, and members of union households found that each of these groups thinks the best way to deal with illegal immigrants in the country is to enforce the law and cause them to return home. Indeed, it seems, the only ones who are fighting enforcement are the influential business lobbying organizations such as the U.S. Chamber of Commerce, the National Restaurant Association, and the National Association of Home Builders, which have all endorsed legalization and increased future immigration. The majority of businesses, especially small businesses, don't agree with the lobbyists.

The Chamber of Commerce's position is just plain appalling. Its stance is that there are not enough Americans to do jobs that require relatively little education. The chamber has testified before Congress that "we face a larger and larger shortage of workers, especially at the low-skilled end of the economy."

This is a lie, as is the contention that entire segments of the economy depend on illegal workers. Bear in mind that this testimony occurred at the height of the recession. That attitude is an insult to American workers and a slap in the face of American law. The same disconnect is played out between union leaders and members, with leaders in favor of legalization and workers staunchly opposed.

A PORTRAIT OF ILLEGAL HIRING

There are two kinds of illegal hiring. The first is due to sloppy standards; companies don't care enough to invest in making sure every employee and every contractor's and supplier's employee is not carrying falsified documents—which are often hard to recognize. If everything looks in order, they'd rather just turn the other way. The other kind of illegal hiring is deliberate, done for one simple reason: the labor is cheaper.

The price of getting caught—a misdemeanor charge and a negligible fine—is often worth the savings in employee salary and benefits. Illegals are wonderful employees for Mr. Scrooge. They work long hours for less than the minimum wage; don't complain about not having time off; require no health insurance or other benefits; and tolerate safety violations, sexual harassment, and other conditions that American workers don't. As an extra bonus, many illegals are paid in cash under the table, so there isn't even a Social Security tax burden for the employer.

But as we've pointed out before, illegal labor isn't really so cheap. I've heard the argument that even illegals pay taxes, and this is true, but that those receipts don't even come close to equaling the expenditures. On the state and local levels, where most of the cost is incurred, less than 5 percent of the outlay is recouped.

Illegals: The Direct Costs

These are the DIRECT after-tax costs illegal immigrants impose on the public coffers each year.

- $2.5 billion—Medicare
- $2.2 billion—medical treatment for uninsured
- $1.9 billion—food assistance programs/food stamps
- $1.6 billion—federal courts and prisons
- $1.4 billion—education via federal aid to schools

TOTAL: $9.6 BILLION

Source: *Center for Immigration Studies*

The rising income gap in America is precisely why we must plug the immigration dike. The waves of newcomers, mostly from the Third World, make it inevitable that our social services sector will grow and the income gap will become wider. This will affect our nation's ability to compete on a global stage for generations to come. Marcelo M. Suaerz-Orozo, codirector of the immigration research center at NYU, put it bluntly and succinctly: "Today we have two elevators—one stuck in the basement and the other moving up faster than it ever has before," he said. "It is placing us at a huge disadvantage."

Experts have noted for years that there is a "quality" issue with the new population of immigrants. In 1997, a study by the National Academy of Sciences noted that "the skills of new waves of immigrants have been declining relative to that of native-born Americans for decades."

The political debate about what to do about illegal immigration seems circular and heavily rhetorical, with little emphasis on practical solutions. The American public is caught in the middle—ill informed about the scope and the cost of illegal immigration and completely at a loss about how to change it. Clearly, blanket amnesty isn't the solution; in fact, it only makes matters worse.

According to the Center for Immigration Studies, amnesty for illegal immigrants will cause direct costs to increase significantly from $10.4 billion a year to $28.8 billion. This is because an amnesty program would transform an illegal immigrant to an "unskilled immigrant with legal status" who could access various government programs. However, as a result of low income, these "unskilled immigrants with legal status" would likely make very modest tax payments.

THE MYTH OF UNDOCUMENTED WORKERS

Illegal aliens aren't necessarily undocumented, thanks to a thriving industry of identity theft. Many people have the misconception that illegals are walking around without papers and are subject to being caught and deported at any instant. Instead, a majority of them have papers. According to the Center for Immigration Studies, as many as 75 percent of working illegals use fraudulent Social Security cards to obtain employment. Many also have forged driver's licenses, fake green cards, and phony birth certificates. The statistics show that being an illegal alien is not usually a victimless crime. For example, in Arizona, it is estimated that more than one million children are the victims of identity theft because illegals use their Social Security numbers for employment. American citizens with Hispanic surnames are even more likely to be victims of identity theft.

Victims suffer real consequences, even when they are children. There have been countless examples of children being denied Medicaid benefits because their Social Security numbers were already being used. People have been arrested or refused jobs and benefits because of actions of those who stole their identities.

Illegal aliens have learned that it is virtually impossible to live and function freely in America without papers, so they compound the illegality of their entry by creating false papers. While illegals are earning money to support their own children back home, the American children who are victimized in this way are paying the price. It stands to reason that if you enter the United States by breaking the law, you will be more likely to break the law again in order to get documents and game the system.

Restoring American jobs

No longer content to sit by and watch its border communities being flooded by illegal aliens or threatened by violence, the state of Arizona took matters into its own hands in 2010 when Governor Jan Brewer signed the nation's toughest immigration law. The most controversial aspect of the law was the requirement that people carry immigration documents to prove that they're here legally. Critics immediately called it racial profiling, since the majority of immigrants—including illegals—are Hispanic. I have no problem with authorities asking for proof of legality. Let's face it: if Congress had acted on creating a national ID card, as it has been talking about doing for decades, this wouldn't even be an issue. My view of the Arizona bill is that it is not perfect, but we have to start somewhere. In the absence of a strong national plan of action, border states have no choice but to enact their own programs.

Arizona's law notwithstanding, immigration experts don't think a raft of new laws will make much difference, for the simple reason that the laws already on the books are suffering from neglect. If current immigration laws were enforced, Americans could realize an employment boom that might open up as many as eight million jobs. That's the claim of some leading immigration reformers in the U.S. Congress. They are not calling for new laws—simply enforcement of those already on the books. The Center for Immigration Studies suggests that "a strategy of attrition through enforcement, which includes mandatory workplace verification and measures to curb misuse of Social Security numbers, could reduce the illegal population by as many as 1.5 million illegal immigrants each year." We'll discuss these and other solutions in more detail in later chapters, but the point is clear: there are solutions if we have the public will to enforce them.

If the government would take simple and obvious steps to enforce immigration laws already on the books, the jobs picture would improve instantly.

Yet the U.S. Immigrations and Customs Enforcement Agency acknowledges that recent years have seen a substantial drop in workplace enforcement activities. Why? Budget cuts! To the average observer, it looks as if we pay lip service to enforcement yet do nothing.

The amnesty trap

In March 2010, we witnessed a remarkable example of hubris: 60,000 illegal aliens and their supporters marched on Washington demanding amnesty. Flaunting our laws every day, they live in this country and nevertheless feel entitled to the First Amendment rights enjoyed by citizens. What is wrong with this picture?

Amnesty is a favorite cause of open-border advocates who champion the rights of illegals with great fervor, often at the expense of their own constituents. Rarely do we hear any serious discussion of the potential pitfalls or the real costs of amnesty; it is always presented as if it were simply a matter of working out a few kinks.

But anyone who was around for the last big amnesty push will realize that we are once again being sold a bill of goods. In 1986, during Ronald Reagan's presidency, the Immigration and Reform Control Act (also called the Simpson-Mazzoli Act after its cosponsors) gave amnesty to some 2.7 million illegals living in the United States. It stipulated:

> *The Attorney General shall adjust the status of an alien to that of an alien lawfully admitted for temporary residence if the alien meets the following requirements: [. . .] IN GENERAL.—The alien must establish that he entered the United States before January 1, 1982, and that he has resided continuously in the United States in an unlawful status since such date and through the date the application is filed under this subsection. [. . .]—In the case of an alien who entered the United States as a nonimmigrant before January 1, 1982, the alien must establish that the alien's period of authorized stay as a nonimmigrant expired before such*

> *date through the passage of time or the alien's unlawful status was*
> *known to the Government as of such date.*

Reagan, however, saw amnesty as a positive move, and he was supported by Congress. There was hardly a ripple of opposition to Simpson-Mazzoli—quite remarkable in light of the blanket amnesty it proposed. A rare dissent was voiced by Representative Bill McCollum of Florida (now the state's attorney general). McCollum predicted that Simpson-Mazzoli would ultimately cause skyrocketing numbers because each illegal would then be entitled to bring spouses, parents, children, and other relatives into the country. McCollum's estimate: in a decade, the bill could attract up to 90 million new illegals because once you provide amnesty, you create an enduring hope among future aliens that their turn may come some day. (It was an exaggerated number, in my opinion, but McCollum's point was legitimate.) It should be noted that in 1986, U.S. Border Patrol recorded the largest annual number of arrests—1,693,000—as immigrants flooded to the border hoping to take advantage of this amnesty bill. Yet when he signed the legislation, President Reagan ignored the warnings and said, "The problem of illegal immigration should not . . . be seen as a problem between the United States and its neighbors. Our objective is only to establish a reasonable, fair, orderly, and secure system of immigration into this country and not to discriminate in any way against particular nations or people."

Looking back, I wonder whether he would make the same claim today. The goal of the amnesty bill was essentially to wipe the slate clean, to strike what one analyst called a "grand bargain." The thinking—not so different from current amnesty discussions—was that the bill would take care of many immigration policy disputes. Illegals would receive amnesty, but the door would close on benefits to future illegals. This would be accomplished through strict sanctions for employers who hired illegal aliens. With the job spigot closed, the incentive to come to America illegally would cease to exist. It was all quite simple and logical. In the end, the agreement was bipartisan and had the support not only of Reagan but also of his attorney general,

Ed Meese; the leaders of the Republican-controlled Senate; and the leaders of the Democratic-controlled House.

The Simpson-Mazzoli Act ultimately failed, not because it was a bad bill but because the entire enforcement requisite was almost completely ignored. Now, proponents of a new amnesty bill, seeking to embrace some 12 million illegals, are heading down the same road. Basically, they're saying that every 25 years or so we'll have to create new amnesties for millions of additional illegals. How does that make sense?

Writing in *The Washington Post* 20 years after their legislation was passed, the coauthors of the 1986 amnesty bill, Alan Simpson and Romano Mazzoli, were on the defensive, basically saying that there was nothing wrong with their approach—it was the fault of enforcers that it didn't work.

"From 1981, when our bill was introduced, to 1986, when it became law, we were aided by the expertise of hundreds of policy experts, scholars and advocates," they wrote. "Our comprehensive bill was crafted to curtail illegal immigration, to provide personnel for labor-scarce markets and to give the most worthy of our illegal population a chance to earn legal status. The foundation of IRCA was enforcement and border security, but to work, it required consistent funding: for agents to investigate workplace violations, for prosecution of employers who broke the law, for more Border Patrol agents, and for installing the latest in high-tech monitoring and surveillance equipment." Simpson and Mazzoli complained that there never seemed to be enough money or enough political will to make it work. But that's precisely the problem.

Robert Rector of the Heritage Foundation estimates that amnesty will cost U.S. taxpayers $2.6 trillion. "Giving amnesty to illegal immigrants will greatly increase long-term costs to the taxpayer," he argues. "Granting amnesty to illegal immigrants would, over time, increase their use of means-tested welfare, Social Security, and Medicare. Fiscal costs would rise in the intermediate term and increase dramatically when amnesty recipients reach retirement. Although it is difficult to provide a precise estimate, it seems likely that if 10 million adult illegal immigrants currently in the U.S. were granted amnesty, the net retirement cost to government (benefits minus taxes) could be over $2.6 trillion."

Let's consider one aspect of the amnesty program, the DREAM Act—a not-so-sweet dream. DREAM is an acronym for the Development, Relief and Education for Alien Minors Development, and the act has typically garnered bipartisan support in Congress. It provides a path to legalization for illegal children and youth. The DREAM Act has been popular because it purports to help innocent victims—the young people whose parents brought them over and who essentially grew up as Americans. Many of them have no memory of or connection to "back home." Supporters in Congress have been trying to get the DREAM Act passed since 2001, so far unsuccessfully.

But the DREAM Act's popularity is really just a knee-jerk reaction to the specter of victims being unfairly treated. While it's true that these young people are illegally in America through no fault of their own, such a massive amnesty program would come at a phenomenal cost—especially to a small group of states that have proportionately high numbers of illegal immigrants.

In fact, the DREAM Act would set in motion a process for potentially amnestying 2.1 million illegal immigrants, not counting the millions of parents and siblings who would also likely be legalized as a result.

Personally, I agree with the principle that the sins of the fathers should not be visited upon their children. I am even inclined to support the DREAM Act. But it must be decoupled from family reunification so that our good intentions do not bury us under a wave of additional millions of relatives.

HAVING A HEART

Let's return to the topic of compassion. I have had many occasions over the years to speak with illegal immigrants who came to the United States out of desperation. Their stories are both sad and inspiring—sad because too often conditions in their home countries are so bad that they felt forced to leave and inspiring because they will make any sacrifice to increase opportunities for their children. Yet their goals and logic are deeply flawed. It is not unusual for mothers and fathers to leave their children behind for their entire childhoods under the auspices of making more money in America. But what are they really gaining? One of these migrants is a woman named Anna R., whom I met in Washington, D.C.,Anna left her two children behind in El Salvador to work as a housekeeper in the United States. Her life was one of ongoing poverty, loneliness, and struggle. Curious about why a mother would leave her children behind for many years to live a hard life here, I asked Anna to put her story in writing—to explain the reasons she came to America, what she hoped to gain in exchange for the sacrifices she made, and what the United States meant to her. This is her response:

Dear Mr. Sobhani:

I am thirty-seven years old and of Salvadorian nationality. I made the hardest decision in my life and that was coming to an unknown country without permission. I came to America by bus from El Salvador to Mexico, then across the border in Phoenix, Arizona without papers. My journey was bad because anything can happen in a week walking through a desert. A snake could come out of nowhere and bite you! I came to Washington D.C. to live with my uncle and hoped he would help me find a job. I had a driver's license from El Salvador and I took the test and changed it to a Maryland license.

There are several reasons related to my decision of migrating to this country such as: education, economy, and shelter.

I, being a single mother, not having the opportunity to get an education and having the desire that one day my kids could achieve something better than me, made the decision to come to this country to seek a better future not only for me but for my kids as well and leaving them with my mother's supervision. Having to give the responsibility of my children to my mother is not easy because of her diabetes but at least I know that she's taking care of them with the same love and care I would have provided them if I had stayed back home.

The economy in my country is a big problem and the government doesn't provide us with any help. Therefore, everyone looks for opportunities to make money to support their families. In my case, I did not have a choice but to come here and work hard to help my kids with the school and my mother with her illness. In my country, going to college is just as hard as it is in here with the difference that here if a student works hard in school, that student gets help from the government or any other foundation and in my country that doesn't happen even if the student is the smartest of the class. Paying for my mother's medicine is another responsibility that I take on myself and her diabetes makes her even more difficult to take the time to take care of my kids. My dreams are that my kids get a better life, a better future and become successful in anything they decide to do. My wish is to live with my family, something that I haven't got to accomplish because I've been always working away from home. I need money before I can go back. My parents are hardworking, and my father has a job that keeps food on the table and a roof over their heads. I have the hope to have money and go back to my country to be with my family and never leave them again.

Sincerely,

Anna R.

Illegals such as Anna come because they feel they have no choice. Regardless of how we may judge their decision, it is a moral outrage—indeed, a crime—that people have to leave their countries because of corruption, lack of good governance, and repression. It is unconscionable for the United States to remain silent in the face of repression abroad. All of these innocent souls who leave their countries have no advocates at home. The flip side of our failed immigration policy is the failure of our foreign policy to insist on good governance in places such as Mexico, failure to help the people of Iran change the dictatorship of the clerics in Iran, zero tolerance for corruption in countries such as Russia and Pakistan, and to help unfurl the banner of freedom for all.

We have an ethical obligation to speak out loudly and without any hesitation that people who escape their predicament to come to our shores deserve our unwavering dedication to exporting those values—economic opportunity, rule of law—that have made America a magnet for millions. Instead of focusing all of our energies on devising paths to citizenship, let's study what would make it feasible and even desirable for immigrants to desire a path back home.

Meanwhile, I find myself wanting to ask the pro-immigration activists, "What is your endgame?" Do activists want totally open borders, complete amnesty for illegal immigrants, Spanish elevated as the official language? Do they want us to press 2 for English? Nowhere do activists place the blame where it belongs—on bad governance in their home countries. They'd rather play the victim here than fix things back home.

When I interview illegal immigrants and ask them why they come here to lead lives that are not particularly good, they give me two reasons: wages and corruption. We can get a picture of exactly how dire the situation is by taking a trip to the border.

Chapter 3

A Tale of Two Cities

*I fear the carnival of crime
is beginning on our border.*

—Edward Blake

San Diego is an American gem, a beautiful coastal city located in the southwest corner of California. Its motto, *Semper vigilans* (ever vigilant), is meaningful for a proud port city, although its southern border—the busiest international land crossing in the world—is far more porous.

San Diego seems to have it all: stunning vistas, thriving industries, an enviable climate, and a vibrant culture. It is the fifth-wealthiest city in the United States, with growing telecommunications, electronics, computer science, and biotechnology industries. It is also a primary naval port and shipbuilding center, as well as a popular tourist and convention destination, with attractions such as SeaWorld and the San Diego Zoo. In 2009, more than 30 million visitors flocked there.

When visitors fly into San Diego's International Airport, circle over the glistening Pacific Ocean, and look below, a seamless metropolitan area appears to stretch along the coastline. It is only on the ground that it becomes clear that there are two distinct cities, representing entirely different cultures, sitting side-by-side. Directly across the border from San Diego, Tijuana shares the striking natural beauty of its prosperous neighbor, but all similarities end there. Except for a small number of wealthy enclaves, Tijuana reeks of poverty. The border area is jammed with cut-rate pharmacies, restaurants, bars, and clubs. The legal drinking age is 18, three years earlier than that in the United States, thus making it a nightlife draw for young San Diegans. The buildings, fences, and sidewalks of Tijuana are covered with graffiti, mostly gang signifiers, the art form of the lawless.

In the city of 1.8 million, the majority of Tijuana's population is composed of migrants from other parts of Mexico and Latin America. It is impossible to have a stable, well-governed city when most of the residents are transients. Almost 100,000 people move to Tijuana every year. It would be naive to suggest that there is any reason other than its proximity to the United States and the opportunity it provides to get there.

The heart of the issue

One of the central questions of world economics (and of this book) is why some countries, such as the United States, are rich while others, such as Mexico and Central America, are poor. The per capita GNP of the United States is six times that of Mexico. This, in essence, is the difference between San Diego and Tijuana.

This is not just a challenging theoretical question but also one with important policy implications. It is a question seldom asked by those advocating open borders, amnesty, driver's licenses for illegal immigrants, and other such policies. If we can identify the answers, then poor countries such as Mexico and those in Central and South America could concentrate on changing the things that keep them poor and adopting the things that make countries such as America rich.

Human institutions play a major role in what happens in the tale of our two cities—and, by extension, the United States and Mexico. The clearest evidence of this view comes from pairs of countries that divide the same environment but have very different institutions, for example, North and South Korea, West and East Germany before the collapse of the Berlin Wall, Haiti and the Dominican Republic, or Costa Rica and Guatemala. One can argue that Tijuana and San Diego also share the same real estate but are very different.

What does San Diego have that Tijuana does not? Writ large, what does the United States have that Mexico does not? The answer is very simple. The United States (and places such as Costa Rica—in the heart of an impoverished Central America) has effective rule of law, enforcement of contracts, protection of private property rights, lack of corruption, low frequency of political upheaval through assassinations and coups, openness to trade and to flow of capital, incentives for investment, and a relatively good education system.

We cannot tell a tale of Mexico and the United States without also being clear that these factors do not exist across the border.

CROSSING OVER

It would probably surprise most people to learn that it's easy to go back and forth between Mexico and the United States. In most respects, it's no different from the average commute anywhere, with traffic jams being the biggest barrier to access.

The region has three major international ports of entry. The primary border crossing, San Ysidro, is the busiest in the world for both vehicles and pedestrians, with waiting times sometimes exceeding two hours for cars and trucks. Eight miles to the east is the Otay Mesa border crossing, used primarily for commercial traffic. A third border crossing, which accommodates both commercial and private vehicles, is located in Tecate. In the past few years, all three crossings have reported significant increases in traffic, but the greatest of these is Tijuana.

A study by the San Diego Association of Governments (SANDAG), designed to find out why people cross the border, reported that there are 60 million trips over the three crossings each year.

Why They Cross the Border		
Self-Reported Reasons for Crossing	From San Diego to Tijuana	From Tijuana to San Diego
Shopping/Gas	28%	78%
Work	1%	9%
Vacation/Recreation	69%	16%
Study/School	0%	3%
Friends/Family	16%	34%

Source: *San Diego Association of Governments*

Study respondents reported crossing the border for a variety of reasons, including shopping, employment, education, healthcare services, and entertainment. They also cross for business, to work, and for visits with family and friends. For the most part, San Diegans report crossing the border for recreation and vacation, as opposed to necessity. In contrast, more than three-quarters of respondents in Tijuana, Tecate, and Rosarito said they crossed the border for shopping or gas, activities that would occur on a regular basis but not every day.

The self-reporting raises questions, however, about the true reasons Mexicans cross into San Diego. Particularly glaring for me in the survey was the low percentage of people saying they crossed for work. I think we can safely assume that a certain number say they cross for shopping or to visit relatives but are actually employed in the San Diego area without work permits.

I have to wonder what the value of such a survey is when both the survey's creators and the respondents are motivated to lie. Clearly, the government believes it has a stake in showing a vital binational economy, and the respondents have a stake in showing they are law-abiding border crossers. The truth rests somewhere in the middle.

San Diego Mayor Jerry Sanders and Tijuana Mayor Jorge Ramos collude in the happy fiction that their cities form a cohesive whole. But a 2010 report published by Tito Alegria, a professor of urban and environmental studies at Tijuana's North Border College, paints a different picture. The report shows that San Diego's growth has occurred organically as a result of regional and national economic, political, and social conditions. However, Tijuana's growth is almost entirely the result of its border location and the small pieces of prosperity it can siphon off its neighbor.

The most important characteristic of any place is its core identity, and here the two cities present very different profiles. San Diego exists to thrive and prosper and fulfill the American dream. Only 10 percent of San Diegans make the border crossing more than a couple of times a year. Tijuana exists because of the promise San Diego holds as a gateway to America. San Diego could exist economically and culturally without Tijuana, but the reverse is not true. As one

San Diego official put it, "San Diego represents possibility; Tijuana represents problems."

An interesting development has been the sudden increase of Indian nationals trying to enter the United States from Mexico. In 2009, there were 204 Indian nationals seized, and in 2010, there were 975—a 475 percent increase in just one year. They make the journey to Mexico and then enter the United States from the south. Just imagine how many other illegal immigrants—representing countries all over the world—come into the United States each and every day from Mexico and are not apprehended. (India is another country with crushing poverty. Imagine one billion Indians living on our southern border!)

Economic self-sufficiency is a big part of the equation, and statistics tell a story of stability on the San Diego side and one of poverty on the Tijuana side:

- Gross Regional Product
  San Diego: $120 billion
  Tijuana: $5 billion
- Median Income
  San Diego: $3,623 per month
  Tijuana: $906 per month

In spite of its stability and prosperity, San Diego is threatened by the steady influx of immigrants, almost entirely Hispanic. The Hispanic population in San Diego is the tenth largest in the nation, with Hispanic births surpassing Anglo births. In the next 25 years, it is estimated that Hispanics will comprise the largest section of the population—at about 41 percent.

According to the 2010 Census, this trend is rapid and definitive. In the past decade, the population of San Diego County grew 8.5 percent, with an ever-shifting makeup. More than 31 percent of residents are Hispanic or Latino, and for 33 percent, English is a second language.

While I was researching this book, I met a woman who worked at juvenile hall in San Diego. She herself was the granddaughter of immigrants—one set from Italy and the other from Russia—and she had a deep respect for the immigrant experience. However, she was troubled by the new face of immigration and the blight that she experiences every day as part of her job. She was frustrated by how the burden is underreported, noting that she sees the result of poorly educated people flooding into San Diego. "Education is only obligatory in Mexico through the sixth grade," she told me. "Therefore, most illegals are uneducated and from the poorer echelons of society. The end result is that we are importing millions of uneducated parents and kids. This is having a huge strain on local and state budgets in California." In her office, the majority of juvenile cases are Hispanic. "Parents are caught up in jobs and therefore are not around for their kids. This leaves the kids unsupervised and often leading them to gangs. It's just a reality."

I found this woman to be a caring and dedicated worker who felt that her task was insurmountable. "San Diego is fast looking like Tijuana," she said. "The tale of two cities is looking more and more like one city with two stories."

One of the most poignant descriptions of the sad migration was penned by Teddy Cruz, an architect and urban planning specialist born in Guatemala City. Writing in the liberal magazine *The Nation*, Cruz painted a devastating picture of the costs of immigration to cities such as San Diego:

> As the Latin American diaspora travels north, it inevitably alters and transforms the fabric of San Diego's subdivisions. In these neighborhoods, multigenerational households of extended families shape their own programs of use, taking charge of their own micro-economies in order to maintain a standard for the household. The result: nonconforming uses and high densities that reshape the fabric of the residential neighborhoods where they settle. Alternative social spaces spring up in large parking lots; informal economies such as flea markets and street vendors appear on vacant properties. Housing additions in the shape of illegal companion units are plugged in to existing suburban dwellings to provide affordable living.

The areas of San Diego that have been most impacted by this nonconforming urbanism are concentrated in its first ring of suburbanization. The mutation of these older bedroom communities—from rigid, monocultural and one-dimensional environments to informal, multicultural and cross-programmed communities—opens the question: how do we anticipate density? It may be that the future of Southern California urbanism will be determined by tactics of retrofit and adaptation, making the large small.

In addition to immigrants retrofitting a large section of San Diego's older mid-city neighborhoods (the typical post-war Levittowns) with alternative nonconforming structures, other parts of this first ring of suburbanization have been replaced by larger versions of themselves. As new McMansion subdivisions update these older suburbs in San Diego, the first ring of suburbanization is being dismantled, piece by piece. Small bungalows are dismembered and their pieces given away to Mexican speculators. Thus the debris of Southern California's middle-class suburbs is recycled to build the new periphery of Tijuana.

TERROR ON THE BORDER

Human traffic from Mexico northward is only one part of the problem with our porous borders. In the fall of 2010, a half-mile-long tunnel was discovered by U.S. federal agents that led from a warehouse in Tijuana to a house in San Diego. The tunnel contained 30 tons of marijuana.

Then, the day after Thanksgiving, November 26, federal agents announced that they had discovered yet another half-mile-long tunnel—with rail lines and carts to trundle bundled tons of marijuana from Tijuana to San Diego.

How many more tunnels are there yet to be discovered? How will our government battle these powerful drug cartels? At the moment, violent drug gangs from Mexico are winning the war of the borders. Since 2007, the Mexican government has charged 400 border officials with accepting bribes from drug cartels—60 of them in Tijuana. While the crackdowns may signal Mexico's willingness to impose a rule of law, I fear these are merely token gestures.

San Diego is not the only vibrant American city along the 1,969-mile- long Mexican border, nor is it the only one affected by the impact of illegal immigrants swarming across or the extreme violence that is a constant for the citizenry.

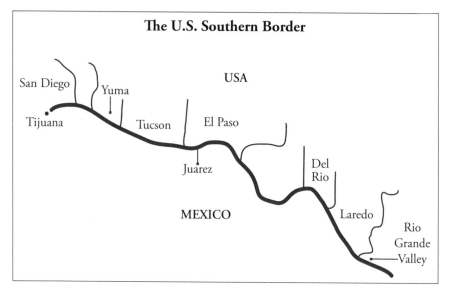

The U.S. Southern Border

Imagine one of the following occurring in any American city or town.

Tijuana, Mexico, November 19, 2010

Two men were slain and hung from a bridge, another was decapitated, and a fourth was shot to death, the result of drug cartel violence. Both victims had their hands and feet bound, and one had his head covered with a black plastic bag. One of the bodies fell into traffic when the rope broke.

A day earlier, a human head was found underneath another bridge in Tijuana, which sits across from San Diego. The body of the 24-year-old man was found 12 hours later alongside the highway from Tijuana to the beach town of Ensenada.

Tijuana, Mexico, October 24, 2010

Armed men burst into a Tijuana drug rehab center and killed 13 recovering addicts. Officials speculated that the killings were in retribution for the seizure of 134 metric tons of marijuana.

Juarez, Mexico, October 22, 2010

In the town bordering El Paso, Texas, 14 people were gunned down at a party.

Juarez, Mexico, November 2010

Four U.S. citizens were shot to death in separate attacks in the border city of Ciudad Juarez. They included a 35-year-old man, a 26-year-old woman, and a 15-year-old boy and girl. All of the murders seemed random and involved several Mexican citizens as well. They might have been drug related.

Such gruesome criminal acts are commonplace in Mexican border towns. Since 2006, an estimated 30,000 people have been killed in drug-related violence in areas along the United States–Mexico border. What would happen if even a fraction of these incidents occurred in San Diego or El Paso? We can well imagine the full power of the federal government, law enforcement agencies, and even the military being brought to bear. Yet, in Mexico, it's a different story. Many experts believe that Mexico has already ceded the rule of law to the powerful drug cartels. They have made a mockery of the laws of both Mexico and the United States and continue to do so because it is tolerated.

Mexico's inability to stem violence has had a deteriorating effect on our own law enforcement efforts. The U.S. Attorneys Annual Statistical Report for Fiscal Year 2009, compiled and released by the Justice Department, is clear evidence that our government is struggling to defend our nation's border with Mexico and protect American citizens. According to the Justice Department's own numbers, crime is dramatically disproportionate along this border compared with that in the rest of the United States. The report also reveals that of the 81,577 defendants convicted in federal court in 2009, 26,538 were convicted in cases the Justice Department categorized as immigration related. Another 26,399 were convicted in drug cases. That means that 33 percent of federal convictions were in immigration cases and 32 percent in drug cases. So, 65 percent of convictions involved Mexican nationals and drug arrests.

"Violence along the border of the United States and Mexico has increased dramatically during recent years," says the U.S. attorneys' report. "The violence associated with Mexican drug trafficking organizations poses a serious problem for law enforcement."

Mexican drug cartels have also taken over some of the drug trade in the United States and are working with several street gangs, according to a report by the National Drug Intelligence Center titled "National Drug Threat Assessment 2009." The threat assessment charges that Mexican drug-trafficking organizations represent the greatest organized crime threat to the United States, and the influence of Mexican drug-trafficking organizations over domestic drug trafficking is unrivaled.

Clearly, the surge in immigration and drug crimes and the concentration of crime at the United States–Mexico border are interrelated; as the report notes, "Illegal immigration provides the initial foothold with which criminal elements, including organized crime syndicates, use to engage in a myriad of illicit activities ranging from immigration document fraud and migrant smuggling to human trafficking."

Since 2009, Marines from nearby Camp Pendleton in California, many of whom are veterans of the wars in Iraq and Afghanistan, have been prohibited from visiting Tijuana without command permission. Why? Because of the rise in gang violence. Those Marines who do receive permission are required to complete antiterrorism training, be given a military security briefing, and employ the buddy system. The irony is inescapable: men and women who have served in the worst war zones in the world are being discouraged from crossing the border into Mexico.

In July 2010, Texas Governor Rick Perry voiced his frustration:

"One look across the border at the gathering storms in cities like Ciudad Juarez, mere miles from El Paso and rapidly devolving into one of the most dangerous cities in the world, and we realize we have a long way to go," he said. "The criminal activity is not limited to areas south of the border; drug cartels and transnational gangs have infiltrated Texas prisons, communities and schools. They work to recruit young people with the promise of fast money and easy living. Unfortunately, the only promises fulfilled by drug cartels are a lifetime in jail or a fast death. A porous border can only lead to more violence. Without border security, there can be no national security."

WHERE'S THE OIL MONEY?

The bitter irony of Mexico's deteriorated state is that, on the books, it has all the elements of a success story: oil and gas; an abundance of natural resources; and good, hardworking people. It is the fourth-largest petroleum producer in the world, after Saudi Arabia, Russia, and Iran. So, where's the money that should be going toward the economic vitality of its people?

Mexico's oil industry is a state-run monopoly, in the hands of Petroleos Mexicanos (Pemex). According to a *New York Times* report, Pemex loses at least $1 billion a year to corruption. In 2011, Mexican auditors found that Pemex improperly awarded $3.1 million in contracts to firms that were unqualified for the task of repairing hurricane damage at a Pemex petrochemical complex in Veracruz. Auditors found "partiality and favoritism . . . toward certain firms in the direct awarding of six contracts." Furthermore, auditors discovered that more than half the contracts they reviewed were awarded without a bidding process to "companies without the experience or financial solvency to execute the contracts."

This might seem like small potatoes for an industry that nets billions every year, but it demonstrates that there is a disregard for ethics up and down the line that leads to a depletion of resources for the state. Pemex accounts for about 40 percent of Mexico's entire revenue.

During the past 40 years, Mexico has produced crude oil, the value of which is conservatively estimated at $1.4 trillion. By this accounting, Mexico should be a wealthy nation whose citizens thrive at home and have no desire to leave. Where is the accountability for the vast resources that are being diverted into the coffers of the few at the expense of the country? Where is the outrage? We must demand justice on behalf of the Mexican people and ask, Where is their $1.4 trillion?

The cost of corruption

A failed Mexico has far-reaching and consequential national security implications for the United States. The narrative of our relations with Mexico should be based on the "soft" power of hope, freedom, and opportunity for all Mexicans *in* Mexico. This can be accomplished by broadcasting live programming into Mexico that highlights what the country can accomplish with good governance. We must demand that Mexico clean its towns and cities of the drug gangs and societal vampires that come along with many desperate people seeking relief. Most illegal immigrants are not concerned about our liberal democratic norms but are focused exclusively on earning a stipend and either saving enough to return home or sending money to loved ones while remaining in the United States. They care about only what they can get from America.

We cannot continue this discussion of Tijuana in a vacuum. The root of all evils flowing north is Mexico's culture of corruption.

There are many who would prefer to gloss over the insidious cost of corruption, to view it as an inconvenience perhaps or, at worst, a moral dilemma to be fixed. But systemic corruption is tantamount to pouring sugar into the gas tank of an economy; once there, it completely destroys the economic engine.

The culture of corruption in Mexico flourishes from the highest levels of government and law enforcement, but it is not just a top-down culture. Bribery is a common exchange system: everything from avoiding a traffic ticket to paying a "tourist tax" for standing on the street. It exists at a level that would be unthinkable in the United States, and yet we've put remarkably little pressure on Mexico to clean it up or be held accountable. The Congressional Hispanic Caucus deals with a lot of issues related to improving the lives of its constituents, but the devastating effects of corruption in Mexico are almost never discussed.

Why is Mexico so corrupt? The dirty little secret of Mexico is that it's an insanely rich country whose wealth is almost entirely in the hands of a few elite families. It was amassed not the "old-fashioned" way but through a lucrative combination of government favoritism and industrial privatization that eliminates competition and reaps hundreds of billions for private companies. The controlling families have little interest in reinvesting those billions inside Mexico, the way iconic American philanthropists such as the Mellons and Morgans gave back here. The bitter irony is that even as poor Mexicans are streaming across the border and American border towns are becoming war zones, the rich owners of business and industry are investing in the United States. Between 1995 and 2005, Mexican capital investment in our country went from zero to $6.7 billion.

This is a form of corporate welfare, Mexican style, with the government providing nontransparent deals to well-connected businesspersons and creating monopolies for the chosen few but leaving average Mexicans behind. In 1960, *Time* magazine declared William Jenkins the richest man in Mexico due to the former's close ties to and non-transparent business connections with influential political figures in Mexico, such a General Maximino Avial Camacho.

Here is a clear case in point: the world's number one billionaire, Carlos Slim, is a Mexican. In 2009 he loaned $250 million to the *New York Times* to save the paper from defaulting on its outstanding debt. Why doesn't anyone talk about his background? How did he accumulate his fortune? Slim began amassing his wealth in the late 1980s and early 1990s as a close compatriot of the corrupt Mexican President Carlos Salinas de Gortari. Salinas (who now lives in exile) was responsible for gutting the integrity of Mexican industry and finance through privatization. Aided by Salinas, Slim was able to gain control of the telecommunications company Telefonos de Mexico, known as Telmex, and then went on to buy ownership in many other important Mexican companies. His monopoly of the communications industry through Telmex was his crown jewel. By the time Vincente Fox was elected on a promise of reform, Slim was so powerful that no one could touch him. Today, he literally monopolizes Mexico, especially in the rapidly growing telecommunication fields. He owns the leading Internet provider, the major cell phone provider, and 83 percent of all landlines.

A lot of people in business and finance admire Slim, saying he was savvy enough to get in on the ground floor of opportunity in Mexico. That's only true if it's acceptable to gain wealth and power through connections to corrupt politicians and corporate welfare or if you view monopolies as a healthy dynamic in a society. Slim could have partially redeemed himself had he invested heavily in rebuilding Mexico, but his charitable contributions have been anemic when compared with those of American billionaires such as Warren Buffet and Bill Gates. In January 2011, he told CNBC reporter Michelle Caruso-Cabrera that donating a sizable portion of his fortune to charity, as those men did, was the wrong way to solve problems. "What we need to do as businessmen is to help to solve the problems, the social problems," he said. "To fight poverty but not by charity." I found the interview somewhat disingenuous. It is not cynical to suggest that he benefits from the status quo. It is also not unfair to say that great wealth in the hands of the few produces a culture of corruption. Look at Russia. Since last year, the number of Russian billionaires has increased from 62 to 101. At the same time, according to a report by Deborah Swallow, a leading authority and lecturer on international affairs, corruption has reached a staggering $300 billion. This amount, which is equivalent to the GNP of Taiwan, is siphoned in bribes from the economy per year and helps put the country in 146th place out of 180 in the Corruption Perception Index. So, if we replaced Russia with Mexico, we would have the same situation on our southern border.

Corruption and, by extension, poverty in Mexico continue to spread, thanks to a long-established oligarchy of corrupt politicians, wealthy Mexican families, and government-run labor unions that promote powerful bosses.

Transparency International, an organization that monitors corruption on a global scale, gives Mexico poor marks on its Corruption Perception Index, along with most Latin American countries. The Corruption Perception Index ranks 200 countries by their perceived levels of corruption on a scale of 0 to 10, with 0 being the most corrupt and 10 being the least corrupt. In 2010, Mexico received a poor 3.1, with many Latin countries being deemed equally or more corrupt: Columbia, 3.5; Venezuela, 2.0; Brazil, 3.7; and Argentina, 2.9. In contrast, the United States ranked among low-corruption nations with a 7.1. Canada received an 8.9.

According to TI, corruption thrives where temptation coexists with permissiveness, where institutional checks on power are missing, where decision making remains obscure, where civil society is thin on the ground, and where great inequalities in the distribution of wealth condemn people to live in poverty. This is an accurate description of the situation in Mexico and many other high-corruption locations around the world.

If the American rule of law, respect for property rights, transparent legal system, and good federal, state, and local government were as familiar to Mexican nationals, Central Americans, Latin Americans, Iranians, and Indians, there'd be no further need for immigration.

In "Corruption and Mexican Political Culture," an article published in the *Journal of the Southwest*, Stephen D. Morris tracked public opinion inside Mexico on the degree to which corruption factored into daily life. On the basis of the experiences of officials and citizens, Morris found that a culture of corruption develops over time, as repeated instances cement themselves into the public mentality. Trust weakens; suspicion and cynicism grow. Attitudes become entrenched, especially the belief that bribery or kickbacks are just a way of life, a necessary evil, intractable and defining.

Some results from Morris's surveys:

- More than 70 percent of respondents claimed that "almost everyone" or "many" in government were corrupt.

- 39 percent of businesspeople said that businesses like theirs made under-the-table payments to influence laws, policies, and regulations.
- 60 percent of businesspeople said that acts of corruption within the areas they supervised were "frequent."
- 62 percent of respondents in Mexico City said that at times it was necessary to pay a bribe to resolve a problem.

How tragic that a nation of Mexico's grand history and human achievement has deteriorated so dramatically. We all pay the price for the failure of its laws, the lack of moral integrity that has infused itself into its culture. Because Mexico is our neighbor and its sickness bleeds into our own land, we have a responsibility to help it get better. While we have been so busy in recent years enforcing regime change and exporting our democracy—and our military—to distant places, we have neglected our neighbors to the south, those who will have the greatest influence on our future. One of our biggest strategic mistakes after 9/11 was the decision to invade Middle Eastern countries in search of terrorists. Our expensive efforts to invade Iraq and topple Saddam Hussein and invade Afghanistan to defeat the Taliban have morphed into nation-building efforts costing billions annually and yielding little visible reward. These efforts could have been accomplished by covert action. Meanwhile, our neighbors to the south are starved for attention and support. Mexico deserves better from Washington.

Chapter 4

Blacks Left Behind

Cast down your bucket where you are.

—Booker T. Washington, in an 1885 appeal
to industrialists to hire blacks at home instead
of bringing immigrant labor from abroad

On a recent trip to Houston, at the airport I got into a taxi that was driven by a black gentleman in his 50s. As we maneuvered into traffic, he asked me, "Where are you coming from?" I told him Washington, D.C., and he immediately launched into a diatribe against black politicians. "All those guys up in Washington do is talk about race and victimhood," he said, referring to black congresspeople. "I don't have time for it. Show me a black leader that gives me a job. Show me a black leader that gives me a good education." He reserved special derision for his own congressional representative, Sheila Jackson Lee, a black woman and a member of the Congressional Black Caucus. "As far as I can see, she talks out of both sides of her mouth, pretending to represent blacks while she's throwing open the doors to aliens who are taking our jobs," my driver said.

I asked him to elaborate on the ways immigrants were jeopardizing black employment. "You see this cab?" he asked. "I'm one of the only black cab drivers in this area. There used to be a time when there were a lot of black cab drivers. Now they're all immigrants—from India, Pakistan, Africa, South America. We're being forced out of the workplace, and that's a fact. And the black politicians in Congress, who say they have our best interests at heart, would rather talk about the civil rights of illegal aliens than improving black employment. It's a real shame."

My cab driver was something of an amateur economist. "I've got nothing against any people trying to make a living," he said, "but it's very simply the law of supply and demand. There are only so many jobs, and if we're putting out the welcome wagon to foreigners before we take care of our own, that's a problem."

As I went about my business over the next few days, I couldn't get his words out of my mind. I realized that in the nation's underbelly, where such conflicts were rarely spoken of openly, there were deep-seated fears and resentments that only grew stronger during economically troubled times. The conflict was not so much between the haves and the have-nots as between the aspirations of various populations vying for any kind of economic power. I couldn't help noticing during my trip that I never again had an African American cab driver, nor did I see African American workers at the construction sites I passed; they were mostly foreign-born Hispanics, as were the workers in my hotel.

Racial discussions are hard to have in this country, where the old wounds of discrimination still fester. As I explored the immigration issue, it became glaringly apparent that our nation's policies are especially devastating to the black community. Still, I resisted posing the issue as black versus brown. It seemed simplistic to say that for every brown person (immigrant) who was employed, a black person was not employed. However, with unemployment numbers at a crisis level, that's the way it appeared.

I know there are those who would say that if black people are unemployed, undereducated, and stuck in a cycle of poverty, it's their own doing. These people bolster their argument by pointing to successful immigrant populations, particularly Asians, that have managed to conquer barriers of language and culture to outperform blacks by most measures. I believe this is a false equivalency. Immigrants of every background came to this nation by choice in order to better their lives, while blacks came by force to lead lives of slavery. The legacy of slavery and discrimination persists today, almost 50 years after the Civil Rights Act.

I was curious about where the Congressional Black Caucus stood on the critical issue of immigration. The CBC, which was officially established in 1971 on a motion by Charles Rangel of New York (a precursor, the Democratic Select Committee, was created in 1969), stated its mission as "positively influencing the course of events pertinent to African-Americans and others of similar experience and situation, and achieving greater equity for persons of African descent in the design and content of domestic and international programs and services." I wondered how true the CBC had remained to its purpose. Were the members of the CBC now supporting measures that placed their core constituencies in economic jeopardy? When I researched the stances of leading members of the CBC, I found that they were overwhelmingly in favor of open borders, amnesty for illegals, and a general policy of tolerance toward immigration. Given the fact that the flood of immigrants, be they legal or illegal, has a devastating effect on black employment, how could the CBC be in favor of more immigration?

"We are all God's children. We all come from somewhere," Texas Congresswoman Sheila Jackson Lee said in defense of her advocacy for open borders. As one of 43 members of the CBC in 2010, she joined her colleagues in calling for amnesty for illegal aliens.

CBC members like to frame the issue as one of civil rights for all people of color. It's a nice sentiment, but that doesn't fully explain why they would advocate so passionately for open immigration when it is an undisputed fact that the policies would mean adding more people to vie for jobs traditionally held by blacks.

When I reviewed the records of key border state congresspersons who were members of the CBC, I found an across-the-board proimmigration philosophy in action. In fact, the lobbying group U.S. Border Control, which is dedicated to ending illegal immigration by securing the borders and reforming border and immigration policies, ranks key CBC members at rock bottom regarding their interest in responsible governance of our nation's borders:

- California Congresswoman Barbara Lee: 0%
- California Congresswoman Laura Richardson: 0%
- California Congresswoman Maxine Waters: 0%
- California Congresswoman Diane Watson: 0%
- Texas Congresswoman Eddie Bernice Johnson: 0%
- Texas Congresswoman Sheila Jackson Lee: 0%
- Maryland Congressman Elijah Cummings: 0%

One explanation for this seemingly inexplicable ranking might be that districts of CBC members such as Sheila Jackson Lee, which were once majority black, have changed in recent years as a result of an influx of Hispanics.

The Hispanic population in Jackson Lee's 18th District now stands at nearly 42 percent.

The same holds true for Maxine Waters, who represents South Central Los Angeles. In 2010, Waters spoke out against building a border fence and reporting illegals who sought medical treatment. It is notable that Waters's district, once majority black, is now only 34.1 percent black and 47.4 percent Hispanic.

A similar story is being repeated in key northern districts, such as the one represented by Charles Rangel. Rangel has represented Harlem since 1971, and it is still the poorest district in America. Why? This is a giant scam perpetrated by CBC members, whose continued failure to reap any economic benefits for their districts is outrageous. Don't tell me the reason is racial prejudice. I don't buy that anymore. Look around. We've got a black president. The richest woman in America, Oprah Winfrey, is black. We're running out of excuses. The tragedy of the black community is that it is being let down by its leaders.

These changing demographics, especially in border states, have been accompanied by a shift in support away from issues of concern to blacks to issues of concern to Hispanics. A big one is immigration.

On a national level, even Barack Obama could not resist the lure of new Hispanic voters when he stated during the 2008 presidential campaign that he didn't believe illegal immigrants were hurting black employment. He actually called the issue a "gimmick." In this case, political expediency trumped common sense and honesty. Even as blacks voted overwhelmingly for Obama, they were being pushed further down into second-class citizenship.

The late black broadcaster Terry Anderson became famous for expressing the rage of the black community toward interlopers that would steal its future. For 10 years (until his untimely death in the summer of 2010), Anderson spoke out against the crushing effects of immigration on his community, calling himself "the prisoner of South Central Los Angeles" and using the tagline "articulating the popular rage." He liked to say, "If you ain't mad, you ain't payin' attention."

Proudly dressed in the blue-collar overalls of the auto mechanic, Anderson gave voice to the frustration and despair felt by black laborers who increasingly watched their livelihoods disappear in the wake of the latest immigration surge. Of the pro-immigration lobbyists, he said, "They won't tell you how skilled black workers in Los Angeles can no longer apply their trade. Body and fender, roofers, framers, drywallers, gardeners, and now even truck drivers . . . We, black Americans, are being displaced in Los Angeles. We are being systematically and economically replaced. And the next time somebody tells you that illegals only take jobs that blacks won't do, just remember that *we* were doing those jobs before the illegals got here."

With Anderson's death, a powerful voice was silenced. Meanwhile, Maxine Waters, his congressional representative, ran for reelection on a pro-immigration platform. The time has come for blacks in the United States to stop automatically voting for leaders who don't support them.

THE TRILLION-DOLLAR HEIST

Peter S. is a lifelong resident of Tobytown, a tiny black enclave in Potomac, Maryland, a mile from my home. With only 60 residents, Tobytown is small, but its historic impact is substantial. The land was purchased in 1875, right after the Civil War, by former slaves, and many of the current residents are direct descendents of those families. For much of its history, Tobytown consisted of tar-paper shacks, even as an affluent neighborhood grew up around it. In the 1970s, federal grants allowed modest middle-class duplexes and single-family homes to be built, and the expectations for the residents of Tobytown were high. Today's recession has toppled many of those dreams.

Peter, a husband and father of two, has worked in the construction industry since 1992, a stable profession in the midst of record housing and business growth. A skilled carpenter, he was once in great demand. However, with the recession bringing the construction industry to a halt, he found it increasingly hard to find work. When I met him in the fall of 2010, Peter had been out of work for a year and a half. Although housing and the construction industry were beginning to make a comeback in the area, he was having trouble getting hired.

"People are working, just not me. The construction sites are full of Hispanics," he said. "People tell me they work cheaper. Are they illegal? I know they show papers, but I can't say whether the papers are legit. Most of us who are out of work suspect our old jobs are being filled by aliens. But even if they're legal, why should immigrants get favored for jobs we've held for years?"

It bears noting that my senator, Barbara Mikulski, has been in office for more than 30 years and always gets reelected by a huge margin. But when you see the deeply ingrained face of poverty in Maryland, you have to wonder what she's doing. Taking the train to New York from Washington, D.C., I am always struck by the view while passing through Baltimore. It looks like a war zone, with shantytowns worse than those in any third world city. Not surprising, Mikulski has a perfect pro-immigration record.

Shortly after I met Peter, I came across a demonstration in downtown Washington, D.C. Around 50 black carpenters—all members of the United Brotherhood of Carpenters—were protesting the use of illegal aliens by a company called Tricon Construction in Laurel, Maryland. I stopped to chat with the protesters. They told me that the company pays illegal workers up to $7 an hour less, turning a blind eye to forged or fraudulent papers and giving blacks the shaft in the process. Also, these folks told me that the company issued 1044 forms for these illegals and then somehow wrote it off on their state and local taxes in a massive misclassification fraud that is going on across the country.

Watching these men and women, hardworking, skilled union members, stand in the cold and fight for their right to a job, I felt furious. I knew I was witnessing a deep injustice. Forty-some years of promises to our black citizens have not been backed up with action. The new civil right should be the right to a job!

The dollars lost to the black community are not a figure out of thin air. Since 1990, if all eligible blacks were employed at an average salary of just $20,000, they would have earned more than $1 trillion in wages. The numbers don't lie when it comes to showing how black workers are being squeezed by immigration policies:

- Black unemployment is 17.6 percent—a full eight points higher than the national average.
- The median household income of blacks is $32,000, compared with $37,000 for illegal immigrants.
- Only one in three blacks ages 16–24 is employed, compared with more than half of whites in the same age group.
- A 2010 report from the Children's Defense Fund finds that about one million black children are living in extreme poverty—a 40 percent increase since 2000.

A Troubling Equation:
The Black Community's Lost Potential

1986

Black population: 29 million

Black workers with capacity to earn $20,000 on average: 17 million

Total earning potential: $340 billion

1996

Black population: 33 million

Black workers with capacity to earn $23,000 on average: 21 million

Total earning potential: $483 billion

2010

Black population: 40 million

Black workers with capacity to earn $30,000 on average: 28 million

Total earning potential: $840 billion

If we take 1986 as our average, then for 24 years (from 1986 to 2010), black net worth from earning should have been $8,160,000,000,000

(i.e., $8 trillion). If we factor in a 30% tax rate, the U.S. Treasury would have collected close to $2.44 trillion in taxes. And if we assume a 5% local tax rate, black communities around America would have been the beneficiaries of a $400-billion injection into schools, parks, neighborhoods, and medical facilities

The above figure is what would have been poured back into the black communities and lifted the entire boat. If our government had done its job and limited immigration since 1986 and given those jobs to blacks at average wages, the black community's net worth would have been $8 trillion.

Every once in a while, a company that thumbs its nose at federal law and hires illegals gets exposed, and the outcome is good for blacks. One example is the North Carolina poultry producer House of Raeford. In late 2008, it came to light that one of its subsidiaries was knowingly hiring illegal immigrants. Customs officials raided the plant and caught 300 illegals, which led the entire company to rethink its hiring policies. It began hiring American-born labor. According to *The Charlotte Observer*, a year after the raid, the House of Raeford's major production line in Raeford, North Carolina, had gone from 80 percent Latino to 70 percent black.

I wonder how many factories and production lines harbor illegals at the same level. Imagine what a national effort to enforce our laws would accomplish for black Americans!

In his April 5, 2008, testimony before the U.S. Commission on Civil Rights, Steven Camarota of the Center for Immigration Studies pointed to several studies that have found that immigration has impacted the wages or employment of native-born African Americans. In clear and direct words, Camarota told Congress:

There are a number of studies indicating that immigration is harming the labor market prospects of black Americans. However, the debate over whether immigration reduces wages or employment among black Americans is not entirely settled. If one is concerned about less-educated workers in this country, it is difficult to justify continuing high levels of legal and illegal immigration that disproportionately impact the bottom end of the labor market.

More than two years later, it would appear that Camarota's testimony made no impact whatsoever on the legislative direction of Congress, in large part because the representatives who care most about black opportunity are hesitant to alienate their growing Hispanic constituencies.

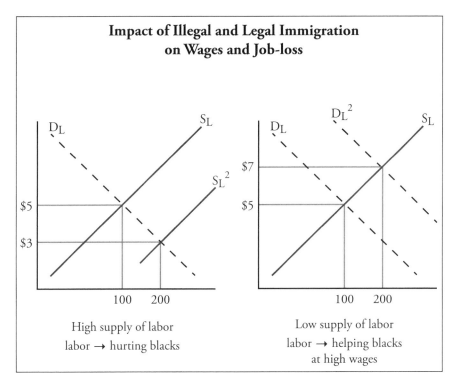

Impact of Illegal and Legal Immigration on Wages and Job-loss

High supply of labor
labor → hurting blacks

Low supply of labor
labor → helping blacks
at high wages

A LONG STRUGGLE FOR ECONOMIC EQUALITY

The issue of dignity and justice for blacks has a long history. There is much unfinished business with the black community in America. A terrible injustice was done with slavery, and the injustice didn't end after the Civil War. It continued well into the second half of the twentieth century, and in economic terms it continues to this day. I believe that we owe the black community more than we owe any other group, but this has never been a widely held perspective. Immigrants' claim on black jobs is an old battle, and usurping black prosperity through immigration is a centuries-old practice. Emancipation of the slaves was followed by the greatest wave of immigration since the birth of this country. Few accounts of the "Great Wave" presented it as anything other than a miraculous and wondrous force for prosperity. Its dampening effects on the fragile black foothold are seldom discussed. Even before Emancipation, conditions in the North had been set against free blacks for decades. In the 1850s, the former slave Frederick Douglass warned that immigrants were replacing black workers and pushing them further down the economic scale. Immigrant populations tended to organize themselves ethnically, excluding others. For example, Irish unions that controlled northeastern waterfronts shut out black workers. The issue for many blacks was thus not one of freedom versus slavery; it was whether freedom was fully granted or just a label that held no currency.

In an 1895 address to the Atlanta Exposition, the black leader Booker T. Washington called upon industrialists to halt the flood of immigrants who were displacing blacks in factories. He told the story of a ship lost at sea whose crew was dying of thirst. When the ship was finally sighted by a rescue vessel and sent the SOS that its members were in desperate need of water, the rescue vessel signaled back, "Cast down your buckets where you are." The lost ship's captain had been unaware that they had drifted to the mouth of the Amazon River, where the water was fresh.

Washington exploited the imagery in telling industrialists to halt their recruitment drive for workers from abroad at the expense of the black citizenry at home:

> *To those of my race who depend on bettering their condition in a foreign land or who underestimate the importance of cultivating friendly relations with the Southern white man, who is their next-door neighbor, I would say: "Cast down your bucket where you are."*
>
> *Cast it down in agriculture, mechanics, in commerce, in domestic service, and in the professions. Our greatest danger is that in the great leap from slavery to freedom we may overlook the fact that the masses of us are to live by the productions of our hands, and fail to keep in mind that we shall prosper in proportion as we learn to dignify and glorify common labor and put brains and skill into the common occupations of life . . .*
>
> *To those of the white race who look to the incoming of those of foreign birth and strange tongue and habits for the prosperity of the South, were I permitted I would repeat what I say to my own race, "Cast down your bucket where you are." Cast it down among the eight millions of Negroes whose habits you know, whose fidelity and love you have tested in days when to have proved treacherous meant the ruin of your firesides. Cast down your bucket among these people who have, without strikes and labor wars, tilled your fields, cleared your forests, built your railroads and cities, and brought forth treasures from the bowels of the earth, and helped make possible this magnificent representation of the progress of the South. Casting down your bucket among my people, helping and encouraging them as you are doing on these grounds, and to the education of head, hand and heart, you will find that they will buy your surplus land, make blossom the waste places in your fields, and run your factories.*

Washington's impassioned plea went largely unheeded.

The civil rights struggle of the 1950s and 1960s occurred in a period of relatively light immigration. Not sensing a threat, civil rights leaders such as Martin Luther King Jr. embraced immigrants as sharing a common struggle with the black community. King was a vocal supporter of Cesar Chavez and wrote to him in 1965, "Our separate struggles are really one—a struggle for freedom, for dignity, and for humanity." That same year, King enthusiastically supported proimmigration legislation by saying it was an important civil rights measure because it changed practices that favored immigrants from some countries over others. The late Senator Edward Kennedy, then chairman of the Senate Immigration Subcommittee, said, "The bill will not flood our cities with immigrants. It will not cause American workers to lose their jobs." His promise may have been true for the short term, but the long-term consequences would prove devastating to struggling black workers.

Since 1986, nearly 30 million legal immigrants have come to the United States, along with many millions of illegal aliens. The competition for jobs has increased exponentially. Economists at Northeastern University have found that businesses are substituting immigrants for young American workers, especially for young black men. Some researchers have estimated that immigration has been responsible for one-third of the drop in employment among black men and some of the increase in incarceration. It is a shame that we have more black men in jail than in college.

Even as the toll was rising, black leaders refused to acknowledge it. In the early 1980s, Jesse Jackson picked up the narrative that nonwhites shared a common cause. His "rainbow coalition" of black, brown, red, and yellow was meant to signal a new political era where power was achieved by finding commonality in diversity. Jackson ran for president in 1984 under the rainbow coalition banner, but Hispanics broke away to vote for Walter Mondale. That Hispanics did not see themselves aligned with blacks and other minorities might have sounded a warning alarm to black politicians, but they failed to listen. For the next 25 years, these politicians continued to cater to Hispanics as part of their minority coalition, long after Hispanics had left the building.

To this day, Hispanics are up for grabs as a voting block, shifting their loyalties between parties, depending on who supports their agenda.

Whether because of ideology, pragmatism, or self-interest, the Congressional Black Caucus became one of Washington's most vocal groups opposing immigration restrictions, and it expected its black constituencies to go along. But this didn't always happen. In the California vote on Proposition 187, a 1994 ballot initiative that banned government benefits for illegals, blacks showed a surprising resistance to the official position of black leadership and aligned with whites to support the measure 58 percent to 36 percent, while Latinos generally opposed it. It was an early sign that blacks were willing to fight back. It may also serve as a lesson for independent candidates, and even Republicans, that they face a historic opportunity to realign our political system with black support.

THE TWISTED LEGACY OF BIRTHRIGHT CITIZENSHIP

In 1868, with the adoption of the Fourteenth Amendment to the Constitution, all persons born in the United States achieved automatic citizenship. This right is referred to as *Jus soli*—"the right of the soil." It was a landmark civil rights act, following on the heels of the Thirteenth Amendment, which abolished slavery and whose fundamental purpose was to assure the rights of the newly freed blacks. How ironic that the Fourteenth Amendment is now being used to justify birthright citizenship to any alien, legal or illegal, who happens to be born here.

"My great grandfather was a slave in the state of Louisiana," Terry Anderson once told his audience. "And one of the great moments in our history was the day we were emancipated, but we still had to have something passed that said, officially, we were no longer property, we were now citizens, and any children born to us were citizens. The Fourteenth Amendment was written for my ancestors. Today we've got a new misinterpretation of it that everybody from the world has used to come here and have babies that make them American citizens. It is wrong. It is a misinterpretation. And it angers me personally because it was written for my ancestors and now it is being misused. I am suffering from that and my kids and my grandkids are going to suffer because they took an amendment meant for us and turned it around against us."

Anderson had a point. Common sense would dictate that the circumstances of a foreign child who happens to be born here to noncitizen parents, either deliberately or accidentally, is far different from the status of a black person recently emancipated from slavery and owed the dignity of citizenship. In our quest to confer equality upon blacks, why do others automatically deserve the same treatment?

Indeed, in what other democratic nation does birthright citizenship exist? The United States stands alone among developed nations in offering birthright citizenship without any strings. Even Canada, which has long had an open policy about conferring citizenship upon those born there, modified its laws to exclude the children of illegal aliens. Nations that do not automatically grant citizenship to anyone, legal or illegal, born on their shores include Australia, the United Kingdom, France, Italy, Germany, Ireland, and India.

I can't, for the life of me, imagine why the United States is so resistant to making a simple modification that would deny citizenship to the offspring of illegals. Yet on this matter, black politicians and Hispanic advocacy groups have formed an unhealthy coalition. Black leaders have passionately argued that any change in the protections under the Fourteenth Amendment would be a slap in the face to blacks, but why is this so? In this instance, black leaders are speaking from fear, and they are not acting out of the courage of conviction, to the detriment of a community looking for leadership. The issue here is not black versus brown. Both sides deserve justice—blacks from our government and Hispanics from their home countries.

A CRY FOR JUSTICE AND JOBS

When I talk to average black citizens, it becomes clear that the new civil rights issue is jobs. With a job come dignity, stability, and power. You can't have a place at the table without a job. The conflict between native blacks and immigrant populations vying for jobs isn't strictly a numbers game; it's also an attitude game. Time and again, studies have shown that when given the choice, employers show preferential treatment to immigrants. One study by anthropologists Katherine Newman and Chauncy Lennon of fast-food jobs in Harlem found that immigrants were much more likely to get hired than native-born black Americans. Walk into any Chipotle in Montgomery County, Maryland, and you will not find a single black person working in the restaurant. Or drive along Virginia's Route 7 and walk into any McDonald's. You will be hard pressed to find a black employee.

"To be blunt, a lot of employers would rather not deal with black American workers if they have the option of hiring a docile Hispanic immigrant instead," observed Mark Krikorian. In particular, he said, illegals can be extremely attractive to budget-conscious businesses. "They are not going to demand better wages, and they're not going to ask for time off. And frankly, a lot of bosses are thinking, 'I don't want to deal with a young black male.'"

A long-term study of Los Angeles janitorial services shows that entire categories of jobs once held primarily by blacks have been completely taken over by other minorities. The Government Accounting Office showed that between the late 1970s and 1985, several small firms hired more Mexican janitors at low pay, which prompted building owners to drop contracts with the companies that employed blacks in favor of the cheaper labor source. Industry wages during that period slipped by about a dollar an hour, and the number of black janitors declined from 2,500 to 600. Today, janitorial services in Los Angeles are staffed almost entirely by immigrants.

With legal and illegal immigrants primarily employed in low-wage, low-skilled sectors of the economy, it is no surprise that blacks would be disproportionately affected, especially during recessions, when this sector is particularly hard-hit.

In a 2006 research paper called "Discrimination in Low-Wage Labor Markets," Princeton sociologists found that equally qualified black applicants to low-wage jobs were 10 percent less likely than Latinos to be hired or asked back for second interviews, and employers were twice as likely to prefer white applicants to equally qualified blacks. This statistic is particularly discouraging because it shows that patterns of racism so deeply embedded in American society have survived to this day.

The battle over quotas for public-sector jobs is also a glaring example of how immigration is turning the race-based policies of the past 40 years, originally designed to help blacks, against them. Claude Anderson, head of the Harvest Institute, an advocacy organization for American blacks, believes that the civil rights movement is experiencing a deep betrayal, as immigrants are not held to the same standards as blacks. He points out that immigrants have never been systematically excluded from opportunity or denied their constitutional rights, as blacks have been. Yet the hold-all identification of "minority" provides equal access to outsiders who have not fought the same bias as blacks. There is a fundamental unfairness to a system that puts all minorities in the same boat.

In May 2007, T. Willard Fair, president and CEO of the Urban League of Greater Miami and a board member of the Center for Immigration Studies, made a riveting case to the Congressional Subcommittee on Immigration, Citizenship, Refugees, Border Security, and International Law Committee on the Judiciary. He was there, he told them, to fight for black jobs, which he had been doing his entire adult life. And so he asked:

> *If there's a young black man in Liberty City, where I live, who's good with his hands and wants to become a carpenter, which is more likely to help him achieve that goal—amnesty and more immigration, or enforcement and less immigration?*
>
> *Which is more likely to help an ex-convict or recovering addict get hired at an entry-level job and start the climb back to a decent life— amnesty and more immigration, or enforcement and less immigration?*
>
> *Which is more likely to persuade a teenager in the inner city to reject the lure of gang life and instead stick with honest*

*employment—amnesty and more immigration, or enforcement
and less immigration?*

There is a hardened animosity between blacks and Hispanics that makes
any talk of a coalition feel hopeless. Frank Morris, former dean of graduate
studies at Morgan State University in Baltimore, notes that in studies, "immigrants actually tend to say they think of themselves more like whites in America
than like blacks, which is one reason why a black-brown political coalition has
never existed anywhere except in the minds of black political leaders." Morris, the former head of the Congressional Black Caucus Foundation, accuses
elected black leaders of mining for votes and supporting Hispanic causes out
of fear of losing their jobs.

Yet, in the face of a growing disconnect with black leadership on the
subject of immigration, voices in the black community have begun to emerge
to forcefully reclaim their rights and opportunities.

Earl Ofari Hutchinson, an author and political analyst whose blog,
The Hutchinson Political Report, focuses on issues of concern to the black population, recently described the ludicrous scenario of the Reverend Al Sharpton
leading a protest march of thousands of people in Phoenix, Arizona, with
banners waving and slogans shouted in the manner of civil rights marches
of old—this time to protest Arizona's new strict crackdown on illegal aliens.
Hutchinson noted that a small group of blacks on the periphery of the march
were waging a counter-protest. Their presence was barely mentioned in the
media, and Hutchinson wrote, "The temptation is to laugh off their pro-
Arizona immigration law countermarch as a comic sideshow, a media attention
grab. After all, Sharpton, President Obama, the Congressional Black Caucus,
all major civil rights groups and nearly all local black Democratic state and
local officials unequivocally champion immigration reform and oppose the
Arizona law." But, Hutchinson warned, the counter-protesters represent an
ever-growing, formerly silent majority of blacks no longer willing to advocate
for their own destruction. Blacks need to hold their leaders accountable.

Here is the outrage: while the black leadership in the United States is advocating for job-killing immigration policies that especially harm black communities, the nations exporting their citizens are among the most corrupt in the world. Maybe these so-called black leaders need to focus on the lack of good governance in Mexico, Central America, and Latin America. They should promote creative solutions that keep these populations in their own countries instead of welcoming them here, where their presence destroys opportunities for blacks.

Chapter 5

Population Insanity

It is not more people that are needed in the world but better people, physically, morally and mentally. This question of raising the quality of our American population must also be taken into account in the question of immigration.

—Agnes E. Meyer, journalist, education advocate, and philanthropist

To waste, to destroy, our natural resources, to skin and exhaust the land instead of using it so as to increase its usefulness, will result in undermining in the days of our children the very prosperity which we ought by rights to hand down to them.

—President Theodore Roosevelt

Population Explosion

According to the Census Bureau, these ten states experienced the greatest growth during the last decade. They are all known to be high immigration states. Pay special attention to the percentages. For example, although Nevada added less than one million people, that number represents an astonishing 35.1 percent growth.

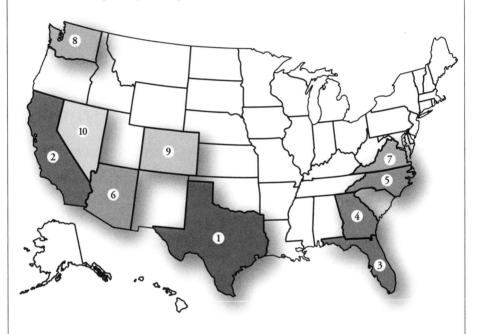

State	Population Increase	Percentage Increase
1. Texas	4,293,741	20.6
2. California	3,382,308	10
3. Florida	2,818,932	17.6
4. Georgia	1,501,200	18.3
5. North Carolina	1,486,170	18.5
6. Arizona	1,261,385	24.6
7. Virginia	922,509	13
8. Washington	830,419	14
9. Colorado	727,935	16.9
10. Nevada	702,294	35.1

O verpopulation is a key attribute of most failed nations, yet we have allowed the U.S. population to double in the past 50 years, with much of that increase due to immigration. That's alarming. We are losing control of our population right before our eyes.

If we were told that the makeup of congressional districts for the foreseeable future—a practical measure of policy-making power—will be determined not by American voters but by millions of legal and illegal immigrants, would we believe it? The answer can be found in the 2010 U.S. Census.

By law, illegal immigrants must be counted in the census, and the latest report includes an estimated 10 million illegals. Since congressional districts are lost or added according to population decline or growth, the net effect of so many illegals is that certain states—particularly those in the West and South—will add congressional districts. "Literally," said Steven Camarota, "we'll have districts where half the adult population can't vote."

Portrait of a Decade 2000–2010	
New Immigrants:	13 million
Babies Born:	10 million
Subtotal:	**23 million**
Emigration and Death:	−5 million
Net Total:	**18 million**

Here's what the census numbers show: during the past decade, our population grew by 27 million, of which 13 million were immigrants—a number that includes both legals and illegals. When emigration and death are accounted for, the net increase is eight million. Add to that 10 million new babies born to immigrants and the figure jumps to 18 million.

The realignment of congressional districts demonstrates that numbers matter. Here's the count: Texas will add four congressional seats; Florida two; and Georgia, South Carolina, Arizona, Utah, Nevada, and Washington State one each. Meanwhile, New York and Ohio will lose two seats apiece. Eight states—Illinois, Iowa, Louisiana, Massachusetts, Michigan, Missouri, New Jersey, and Pennsylvania—will each lose one seat. The shifts will also have an impact on the Electoral College, adding influence for the states that gain congressional districts.

This increased political clout will come at a price to the balance of our two-party system. Because of gerrymandering (the process of organizing districts to give political advantage to one group or another), these new districts will create "safe" seats for congressional representatives who support the open-borders agenda. This is precisely what is happening in California, where 39 of the state's 53 districts in the U.S. House of Representatives will be Democratic-leaning, up from 33 now. A key goal is to provide safe seats for the growing left-leaning Latino politicians in California. Here again we see the dangers inherent in politicians who would like to expand entitlements to cover more people and our broken immigration system. In short, an uncompetitive election system that provides "safe" districts to career politicians, unaccountable entitlements and a growing population are financially unsustainable.

These population shifts might seem of little significance unless you view them as portents for the future. If trends continue, Census Bureau projections show that we are on track to add 130 million more people to the U.S. population in the next 40 years, primarily as a result of future immigration. It is now in the realm of possibility that our government could be influenced by masses of people who are not here legally.

According to a study by the Pew Hispanic Center, about one of every 13 children born in the United States in 2008 was the offspring of illegal parents, and *The Washington Post* reports that on the basis of the new Census Bureau data, more than one-half of California children are Latino. Indeed, in the past decade, Latinos accounted for more than half of the population growth, to top 50 million people. This growth rate far exceeded earlier estimates in most states.

Latino growth translates into Latino clout, and the leaders of their lobbying groups are well aware of how much they might influence future elections, especially if newly created congressional districts are heavily Latino. Arturo Vargas, executive director of the National Association of Latino Elected and Appointed Officials, told *The Washington Post*, "We know as the Latino community that power is not given away. Power is taken. We know that the increases [in population] are largely due to our community's growth. And we intend to translate that to opportunity for our community to have more fair representation in this country."

One place Latino activists are eyeing is Texas, where two-thirds of state growth over the past decade has been Latino. Latinos want to "own" the four new congressional districts.

Similar efforts are taking place across the country, even in areas that would not have been expected to be so heavily Latino. North Carolina has experienced astounding growth in the past decade—up by about 18.5 percent—largely because of a giant increase in the Latino population, now edging toward one million people. The big draw, in addition to climate, is jobs, especially in manufacturing. North Carolina weathered the recession fairly well, but no state can sustain a stable economy with such rapid, massive growth. So the very factors that have drawn this new population will ultimately bring everyone down.

BIRTHRATE DOWN, POPULATION UP

When the 2010 U.S. Census was published, with its watershed number of 309 million Americans, many people were surprised at how quickly our nation has grown in recent years. In a 40-year span, we jumped from 200 to 300 million. Most perplexing to those who haven't been paying close attention until now was that the numbers could have escalated so much while birthrates have been on the decline.

This is a reality check: were it not for the rising numbers of immigrants, both legal and illegal, the American population would not be growing much at all. In fact, the United States is alone among industrialized nations in its relatively rapid population increase. The populations in Japan and Russia are expected to shrink almost one-fourth by 2050. Germany, Italy, and most European nations are also holding population numbers down with low birthrates.

Population stabilization was a key environmental goal beginning in the early 1970s, and we seemed to be doing very well. Since 1972, we have essentially broken even when it comes to the number of births versus the number of deaths. On the basis of citizen fertility numbers alone, the U.S. population should have stabilized at 255 million in 2020 and then gradually decreased. Instead, we're facing a population explosion based solely on runaway immigration. Keep in mind that although our "official" population is 309 million, some educated calculations put the true number at 327 million. According to experts, estimates of illegals are chronically low, and the Census Bureau regularly undercounts this population. For example, in 2004, Bear Stearns Asset Management used employment and financial data and came to the conclusion that the number of illegal immigrants in the United States may be as high as 20 million. (That was seven years ago, as of this writing, so we might be looking at a real number of 25–30 million.)

How can we grow our economy, provide jobs, keep taxes low, and spur entrepreneurship if we face the tsunami of immigration?

THE TRUTH ABOUT ANCHOR BABIES

Julia A., a 34-year-old Mexican citizen, crossed the border on foot into San Diego, accompanied by her husband, Rodrigo, and her two children, 13-year-old Miriam and 10-year-old Marco. The ostensible reason for this family outing was to go shopping. Julia was nine months pregnant, and anyone looking closely might have noticed the frequent winces and careful gait that suggested the early stages of labor. Within nine hours of crossing the border, Julia was in a San Diego emergency room and was delivering her third child, Carla. Carla was welcomed into the world as a bona fide American citizen.

The question of birthright citizenship has been argued passionately from both sides, as we discussed in chapter 4. But it deserves further exploration in light of the disturbing population numbers. Many people find the term "anchor babies" insulting, but it is also accurate. An infant born in America to illegal immigrants literally becomes the anchor for a huge family windfall that keeps on giving—at taxpayer expense. Currently, there are about 350,000 anchor babies born every year at an estimated cost to U.S. taxpayers of $118 billion. These infants are huge consumers of social services. When an anchor baby is born, the parents are usually allowed to stay in the country. Since they probably have no income (it being illegal for them to work in the United States), the baby is eligible for a raft of services, from housing aid to food stamps to medical care.

The problem is more serious than just a few women walking across the border to give birth. A huge global industry has been built around "birth tourism." A July 2010 *Washington Post* article described a Chinese company that, for $14,750, will arrange for a pregnant Chinese woman to travel to the United States, be cared for in a Chinese-run California maternity center, and give birth there, thus guaranteeing the child U.S. citizenship. Such birth tourism companies are completely legal. In fact, there are no restrictions whatsoever on pregnant women traveling to this country.

The only way to stop the trend is to change the law—something virtually every developed nation has done. In January 2011, Republican Representative Steve King of Iowa introduced legislation that would eliminate the granting of automatic citizenship to babies born in the United States. King's legislation, called the Birthright Citizenship Act of 2011, would require at least one parent to be a U.S. citizen or a legal permanent resident for a newborn to receive automatic citizenship.

Said King, "The current practice of extending U.S. citizenship to hundreds of thousands of 'anchor babies' every year arises from the misapplication of the Constitution's citizenship clause and creates an incentive for illegal aliens to cross our border. The Birthright Citizenship Act of 2011 ends this practice by making it clear that a child born in the United States to illegal alien parents does not meet the standard for birthright citizenship already established by the Constitution. Passage of this bill will ensure that immigration law breakers are not rewarded, will close the door to future waves of extended family chain migration, and will help to bring an end to the global 'birth tourism' industry."

King's bill expresses a commonsense response to the problem. However, he faces steep challenges from advocates for birthright citizenship. The most powerful of these advocates is the Catholic Church. The archdioceses of Los Angeles, Chicago, New York, and other big cities are at the forefront of open borders and giving refuge to illegals. The Church is also, notably, opposed to all methods of population control, thus assuring it a steady supply of members from third world countries. In recent decades, almost all new Catholics have come from Latin America, Africa, and Asia, even as Western "believers" decline. It is not hyperbole to suggest that the Catholic Church's stance toward immigration is self-serving, especially since there is no moral outrage expressed about the violence and corruption in the countries where its numbers are booming. In America, the Church is loud when it comes to giving sanctuary but silent when it comes to speaking the truth about corruption. Maybe that's because 42 percent of all legal immigrants in the United States are Catholic. It is projected that by 2020, more than half of its church members here will have Spanish surnames. The Catholic Church remains the largest religious group in the United States, and while Protestant denominations have seen a decline in membership, that same decline in the Catholic Church has been offset almost entirely by immigrants.

The biblical tradition of "welcoming the stranger" is a convenient backdrop for a policy that boosts Church coffers. The Conference of Catholic Bishops has officially come out for "comprehensive immigration reform," including amnesty for illegals. Open borders is actually one of the fundamental tenets of the Church, which has always encouraged migration to seed the nations of the world with Catholic doctrine. (However, I wonder how the Vatican would feel if it were overrun by illegals—if the pope walked outside and was surrounded by masses of people with their hands out, would the Vatican suddenly turn into an overcrowded ghetto, as its doctrine might imply? Of course not.)

This is a rallying issue for Catholic politicians. In May 2010, then–Speaker of the House Nancy Pelosi, who is Catholic, spoke at a conference of priests, nuns, and activists, telling them that they had an important role to play in immigration reform. She told the audience, "The cardinals, the archbishops, the bishops that come to me say, 'We want you to pass immigration reform,' and I say, 'I want you to speak about it from the pulpit. Some [who] oppose immigration reform are sitting in those pews, and you have to tell them that this is a manifestation of our living the gospels.'"

Those are pretty strong words for a secular politician, and they send a chilling message about the power of pro-immigration alliances that aren't necessarily in the best interests of Americans. I feel that "champagne social-ists" such as Pelosi are living in a bubble if they cannot see the disastrous consequences of this stance. Not surprisingly, when Arizona passed its tough immigration law in late 2010, the Catholic Church led the charge against it.

However, it is particularly disturbing to me that the Catholic Church doesn't do more to fight corruption in Mexico, which is a majority-Catholic country. Instead, it does everything possible to encourage Mexicans to come to the United States, even illegally.

THE REAL CULPRIT: CHAIN MIGRATION

Chain migration is the law of the land. It is also compassion run amok. According to Roy Beck, it is the sole factor that has led our legal immigration numbers to skyrocket from around 250,000 a year in the 1950s to more than one million a year since.

It used to be that an immigrant could send for a spouse and children, which was a reasonable policy of family reunification. But the law changed in 1965, when the definition of "family" was expanded to include other relatives, such as siblings and their families, parents and their families, and adult children and their families. In some cases, these relatives receive preference over the nuclear family.

After the change took effect, the chain of immigrants lengthened to untenable levels—and even so, the warm and fuzzy ideal of family reunification is almost beside the point. I often meet immigrants who have left wives and children behind in favor of brothers with whom they work side-by-side. They may see this as a temporary work situation—make enough money and then return home—but as a practical matter, these sibling households go on for years. The brothers then have the opening to sponsor their own chains of relatives.

By allowing each immigrant admitted to subsequently petition for the admission of parents, siblings and their families, and adult children and their families, Congress has put in place an immigration system that results in virtually unlimited chain migration. The initial policy, the aim of which was to keep families together, has not really achieved that; what it has done is create a loophole big enough to drive a truck through.

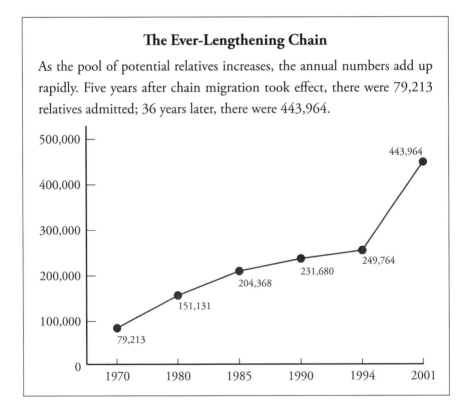

The Ever-Lengthening Chain

As the pool of potential relatives increases, the annual numbers add up rapidly. Five years after chain migration took effect, there were 79,213 relatives admitted; 36 years later, there were 443,964.

As Beck points out, "The claim that chain migration is about family reunification ignores the fact that each immigrant who comes to the U.S. *disunites* another family by leaving some new relatives behind. If a person really wants to live near his/her extended family, he/she should remain in the country where that extended family lives. Except for the very small percentage of each year's newcomers who are refugees, nobody is forcing immigrants to leave their families."

Furthermore, the policy of chain migration worsens the flood of low-skilled, poorly educated immigrants, since entry is based on family ties, not the ability of an immigrant to make a meaningful economic contribution or investment. Just imagine the chain migration impact of amnesty for illegals! Providing that 12 million illegal aliens were given amnesty and a path to citizenship, they would be eligible to apply for green cards and eventual citizenship for their families and extended relatives. If we assume just six relatives each over three years, that is an additional 72 million people! Could we withstand the tidal wave as the families of 10–12 million mostly poor immigrants swept over the country?

IMMIGRATION'S GIANT CARBON FOOTPRINT

There is no question that a spike in population has a terrible environmental impact that includes congestion, sprawl, traffic, pollution, loss of open spaces, and greenhouse gas emissions. Yet when I researched the leading environmental groups, I found that they were completely silent on this matter. The Sierra Club does not even want to look at the question of the carbon footprint of illegal immigrants. None of the organizations wants to touch it. The hypocrisy is stunning. Think about it: if we have 12 million illegal immigrants in America, that's millions of cars, millions of gas and electric expenditures, millions of gallons of water used daily, millions of hours on computers and cell phones, millions of meals consumed, and on and on. The Center for Immigration Studies estimates that if we assume the current ratio of population to infrastructure, adding roughly 30 million people each decade will mean building and paying for 8,000 new schools every 10 years, developing land to accommodate

11.5 million new housing units every 10 years, and constructing enough roads to handle 23.6 million more vehicles every 10 years.

Leon Kolankiewicz, an environmental scientist who conducted a study on the impact of high immigration, found that, in particular, immigration to the United States has a damaging effect because it transfers population from low-polluting parts of the world to a high-polluting area. That is, in America you're more likely to have a car and use other resources to increase your carbon footprint. According to Kolankiewicz, the impact of immigration to the United States on global emissions is equal to approximately 5% of the annual worldwide CO_2 emissions since 1980. In fact, if the 482-million increase in global CO_2 emissions caused by immigration to the United States were a separate country, it would rank tenth in the world in emissions!

Americans are notoriously skeptical about environmental issues, so the carbon footprint problem isn't likely to get much play compared with other immigration problems, but it should. By dismissing the horrific environmental cost of immigration, we are ignoring factors that could lead to our future inability to thrive. Mark my words: there is a direct connection between being stuck in traffic and the immigration-fueled population explosion.

Viewed from the standpoint of the population explosion and its cost to our quality of life and environment, it is insanity to continue current immigration trends. Why should we allow America's superior quality of life to be compromised for the sake of a broken immigration policy?

Colorado State University Professor Philip Cafaro, an expert on environmental ethics, believes the future is dire unless something is done now to stem the population tide. "Like immigration policy for the past 50 years, immigration policy for the next 50 looks likely to be set with no regard for its environmental consequences," he said during a CIS panel discussion. "And I think that's a bad thing. As a committed environmentalist, I'd like to see my government set immigration policy and all government policy within the context of a commitment to sustainability. I don't think the goals I share with my fellow environmentalists and with a large majority of my fellow citizens—goals like clean air and clear water, livable, uncrowded cities, sharing the land with flourishing populations of all our native wildlife species—I don't think these goals are compatible with continued population growth. It's time to rein in this growth or, honestly, renounce the hope of living sustainably here in the United States."

We cannot afford to continue our open-border, pro-immigration policies. Those who advocate that the more people we allow into the country, the stronger we become need to revisit history. At the height of our economic, political, military, and diplomatic powers, the U.S. population stood at 150 million.

An immigration-fueled population explosion comes with an unacceptably high price, but in the many articles published about the 2010 Census, these concerns were rarely voiced. Let's face it. Immigration has become the third rail of American politics—untouchable. We need to speak the truth about how immigration is affecting our country just as we are debating how our mounting debt is crushing us. We cannot afford more people here.

While it is true that immigration made us rich in the past, it is now an economic burden that is stretching our resources.

In short, immigration was the oxygen that once fueled America but the current ill-guided immigration policies are now the cancer that is slowly sapping our national vitality and economic prosperity as a nation.

Chapter 6

The Assimilation Fallacy

I certainly would not be one even to suggest that a man cease to love the home of his birth . . . but it is one thing to love the place you were born and it is another to dedicate yourself to the place in which you go.

—President Woodrow Wilson

More than 100 years ago, Theodore Roosevelt spoke of how crucial national pride and assimilation were to the success of the American dream:

> We should insist that if the immigrant who comes here in good faith becomes an American and assimilates himself to us, he shall be treated on an exact equality with everyone else, for it is an outrage to discriminate against any such man because of creed, or birthplace, or origin. But this is predicated upon the person's becoming in every facet an American, and nothing but an American. There can be no divided allegiance here. Any man who says he is an American, but something else also, isn't an American at all. We have room for but one flag, the American flag. We have room for but one language here, and that is the English language. We have room for but one sole loyalty and that is a loyalty to the American people.

I was raised on the idea of America as a melting pot, and the term used to describe it was *e pluribus unum*—"out of the many, one." The genius of the American system was that it was the first nation devised under a code of commonality through national values, not through birth, status, religion, race, or caste. We may not have shared the same ancestry, but we were nonetheless bound by our magnificent purpose as stated in the Constitution—the entitlement to life, liberty, and the pursuit of happiness. The melting pot of America showed a blending of cultures to achieve a more homogenous whole.

But in recent decades, a new liberal notion of multiculturalism has crept into the lingo and pushed aside the "melting pot" concept. It is considered racist in many circles to refer to America as a melting pot, as it assumes that individual cultures are not fully respected. The new concept, multiculturalism, is more like a mixed salad than a melting pot, with lots of diverse elements contributing their unique characteristics to make a delicious whole. Separate flavors and textures do not blend together but boldly assert their differences. In short, celebrating our differences has taken precedence over accentuating the need for a common narrative.

Multiculturalism presumes a false sameness among cultures and ideals and suggests we're no better or worse than any other country. But is that a valid construct for America, the self-described "more perfect union"? Why pretend that other cultures, value systems, and governments are equal to ours? This country could not have survived its first century if we had not believed it had a unique character that distinguished it from other countries. American exceptionalism is a valid construct: Puerto Rico did not produce Sonia Sotomayor; America did. Russia did not produce Sergey Brin; America did. Iran did not produce Pierre Omidyar; America did. India did not produce Fareed Zakaria; America did. (And yet Puerto Rico, Russia, Iran, and India have talented individuals who can blossom into the next Sotomayor, Brin, Omidyar, or Zakaria, provided good governance becomes the rule and not the exception.) American culture is not superior, but it is certainly exceptional, and it is this culture that defines our national identity and should be a source of pride.

While there are hundreds of thousands of immigrants who have adopted the United States with open hearts, it is becoming increasingly difficult to ask for emotional attachment—some call it loyalty—when new arrivals can so easily go back to their home countries and thus never have to assimilate into the United States. Citizenship or residency without emotional attachment weakens the national ethos.

DUAL LOYALTY

If you've ever attended a swearing-in ceremony for new U.S. citizens, it is a moving and sobering experience. Most of us, having been born here, never have an opportunity to say the oath or know what it entails. I've attended these ceremonies and am always struck by the powerful conviction behind the words:

I hereby declare, on oath,

that I absolutely and entirely renounce and abjure all allegiance and fidelity to any foreign prince, potentate, state, or sovereignty of whom or which I have heretofore been a subject or citizen;

that I will support and defend the Constitution and laws of the United States of America against all enemies, foreign and domestic;

that I will bear true faith and allegiance to the same;

that I will bear arms on behalf of the United States when required by law;

that I will perform noncombatant service in the Armed Forces of the United States when required by the law;

that I will perform work of national importance under civilian direction when required by the law;

and that I take this obligation freely without any mental reservation or purpose of evasion; so help me God.

At the heart of the oath is the promise of fealty—in effect, the pledge to forsake all others. I never hear these words without thinking of my father.

My father had a finely tuned moral code and a deep understanding of the meaning of loyalty. I have seldom seen a man with such a strong sense of national pride and duty. Before he fled Iran, he had been a general. When he was forced out of Iran and settled in America, he refused to become an American citizen, even though he could have. I asked him, "Dad, why don't you become an American citizen?" He told me, "Because I cannot have dual loyalty. I made an oath to serve my country. I can't come here, raise my hand, and go through the sham of saying now I'm going to be an American. I can't. My loyalty is there." He believed until his death that he would one day return to Iran, and he held onto that faith. It was his dream to be buried in Iran.

I learned from my dad that fealty means something. It's not just lip service. Yet, every day, immigrants raise their hands and swear an oath while knowing that their loyalties could be tested.

One clear example of divided loyalty is dual citizenship. How can a new citizen pledge on the one hand that "I absolutely and entirely renounce and abjure all allegiance and fidelity to any foreign prince, potentate, state, or sovereignty of whom or which I have heretofore been a subject or citizen" while maintaining citizenship in his or her country of origin? It seems to me that dual citizenship is incompatible with the American oath. Yet 85 percent of all immigrants to the United States come from countries that allow and even encourage dual citizenship because they think they might have some extra influence in America. For the most part, this is considered a nonissue, but even if there are no practical consequences, it would seem there are huge symbolic issues.

Dual citizenship may have a practical advantage in allowing citizens to easily travel between the United States and their home countries, but it remains a barrier to full assimilation. I would personally prefer a climate that encouraged new American citizens to visit their homelands as ambassadors of their newly adopted country and speak about why America is special and how it can serve as a model for others.

Columnist Georgie Anne Geyer once compared dual citizenship to bigamy, and, in some cases, it is an apt comparison. When Mexico changed its law in 1998 to permit Mexican immigrants in the United States to retain Mexican citizenship, the government was quite open about its reason—which was to give Mexican interests more clout within our borders. One Mexican strategist acknowledged, "We are betting that Mexican Americans who are American citizens will think Mexico first, even to the seventh generation."

A thoughtful and provocative paper by Hudson Institute Fellow John Fonte spelled out some specific actions the U.S. government could take to strengthen the intent of the oath of allegiance. These included sanctions of a year in jail and a $10,000 fine if a naturalized citizen voted in an election of his or her home country, ran for office there, used a passport, or served in the armed forces. The allegiance-promoting program would be supervised by the Department of Homeland Security, and new citizens would be informed that its tenets were serious. These proposals make sense to me as a practical demonstration of loyalty to America.

The endgame?

Open-border advocates range from mainstream groups such as the Council of La Raza to a little-known group called the Reconquista movement, whose design is to take back the states along the southwest border—in effect, to *reconquest*. Sadly, none of these advocates (including Spanish media in the United States) highlight the national malady of places such as El Salvador or Mexico; instead, they seem focused on righting a perceived wrong. For example, Reconquista claims that the United States stole large sections of the southwestern United States from Mexico in the 1800s and it's time to restore them to Mexico. No head-on attack is planned. Warriors will not be descending on the southwest with guns blazing. Rather, the method of conquest is to flood the area with immigrants, mostly illegal, whose numbers will forcibly influence the political and cultural direction of the states. If Mexican immigrants are able to gain control of one or more states, they would then secede from the United States and become a part of Mexico. Jose Angel Gutierrez, a political science professor at the University of Texas at Arlington and a supporter of the cause, recently gave a speech and stated: "We are millions. We just have to survive. We have an aging white America. They are not making babies. They are dying. It's a matter of time. The explosion is in our population."

At first blush, the plan might sound nuts, but it is dead serious. Even if total control and secession never come to pass, the population explosion being created will do enormous damage to America's national fabric and economic well-being.

Radical, racist Latino groups are a fact of life in America, but their advocacy of separateness and victimhood does not help solve the fundamental problems facing some countries in Latin America. For example, the slogan of "*La Raza todo. Fuerra de La Raza nada,*" which means "For the race is everything. Outside the race is nothing," does not help my Home Depot friends in any way, shape, or form. Even some public officials in the Southwest see little distinction between border populations in the United States and those in Mexico. Anglos do Leticia, a Texas state senator from San Antonio with deep roots in the area, told *The Economist,* "Our family was there when it was Spain, when it was France, when it was Mexico, the Republic of Texas, the United States, the Confederacy. Our family's always been in the same place. It's the damn government that kept changing." Astonishing that this remark was made by an American official!

LOVING AMERICA

When we look at immigrant movements such as Reconquista and advocacy groups such as La Raza, we see an opposite set of ambitions that have more to do with strengthening ethnic cadres and their supporters back home than with tackling the more challenging problems of good governance. I find it disheartening that we allow them to flourish in our communities. In recent years, there have been huge demonstrations in our cities that encourage amnesty and open borders. It is interesting what you see at such gatherings: Mexican flags and signs that read "Uncle Sam stole our land." Once again, the finger is pointed at the United States instead of the Mexican government, where the blame belongs.

Stanley Renshon, professor of political science at the City University of New York Graduate Center, wrote, "Citizenship without emotional attachment is the civic equivalent of a one-night stand. The power of the American Creed itself rests on a more basic psychological foundation. That foundation is the set of emotional attachments that often are disparaged and very misunderstood. The bonding mechanisms through which 'pluribus' becomes 'unum' are the diverse emotional attachments that are ordinarily summarized by the term 'patriotism.'"

What is that indelible quality called patriotism? I see it as a mix of belief and sentiment. Loving one's country means trusting that, while not perfect, it is the best country in the world. There is also an emotional component—an affection for the culture, a feeling of warmth and pride when the flag is waving and the national anthem is being sung. Patriotism is present in words and actions, including an instantaneous coming together when we are attacked. Think of the unity and strength in evidence everywhere after 9/11 or after the killing of Osama bin Laden. We didn't have to be instructed or encouraged to show solidarity; across regional and political spectrums, the differences disappeared. It was not unusual to hear "We were all New Yorkers that day," just as we more recently heard "We are all Arizonans" in the aftermath of the Gabriel Giffords shooting. The American people come together in times of hardship and in times of joy. We reach out to each other with uplifting words. It's just what we do. It's part of our identity. At the core of that identity is the narrative of America as the model for unity in diversity—the unity of mankind under one political system. This ideal that different races, ethnicities, religions, and classes can all live in fellowship under the protection of a just government that treats all people as equal is quintessentially American. Unity in the context of America's national fabric does not mean sameness; we can still come from different parts of the world, but if our aim and outlook are not aligned with and supportive of the country in which we live, then the diversity will become divisive.

PART TWO:

REAL IMMIGRATION REFORM IN FIVE STEPS

Chapter 7

A Call for Leadership

*You must do the thing you
think you cannot do.*

—Eleanor Roosevelt

Whaat is leadership? Every president wrestles with this question, but I would suggest that presidential leadership is less about the big, dramatic speeches and more about trying to solve the tough, complex issues that belie easy solutions or facile rhetoric. Immigration is such an issue.

During the past 40 years, there have been many occasions when presidential leadership on immigration was needed, but time and again our presidents failed to deliver. In my lifetime alone, presidents from both parties refused to act every time they were faced with the challenge. Ronald Reagan, whose status among conservatives is iconic, was among the hardiest open-border presidents of our era; he oversaw vast amnesty legislation that has repercussions to this day. President Jimmy Carter was less invested but dangerously benign, barely addressing the issue at all. President Clinton and both Presidents Bush bypassed any meaningful chance at reform. President Obama is pro amnesty and pro–open borders, with no feasible plan for stopping the drain on our resources.

The tradition of modern leadership is to kick the immigration can down the road to the next administration or the next Congress. Telling the truth about immigration—and then acting on that truth—is considered political folly, yet our leaders are called to *do the thing they think they cannot do*. And the cans are piling up fast.

It has been more than 15 years since the federal government actually attempted to tackle systemic change in immigration. Although that effort didn't work out so well (otherwise we'd be in a better position today), the experience is instructive because for the first time in recent history, the government actually considered a substantial reduction of immigration numbers. None other than the powerful liberal standard bearer Congresswoman Barbara Jordan of Texas led the U.S. Commission on Immigration Reform, and it was her voice that was raised the loudest—backed almost unanimously by members of her commission—

to say that chain migration, the visa lottery, and other provisions that flood our shores with unskilled labor are in conflict with the best interests of the nation.

"We disagree with those who would label efforts to control immigration as being inherently anti-immigrant," Jordan said. "Rather, it is both a right and a responsibility of a democratic society to manage immigration so that it serves the national interest."

That's leadership. However, the rest of the story is less inspiring. When Jordan presented the commission's report to Congress, the chamber was held spellbound by the conviction in her sonorous voice, as well as by the refreshing simplicity of her recommendations, which she reduced to four main points:

- Improved border management, focused not just on apprehension but also on prevention. "Apprehensions alone cannot measure success in preventing illegal entries. Our goal should be zero apprehensions, not because aliens get past the Border Patrol but because they are prevented entry in the first place."
- Reducing the magnet that jobs provide for illegal immigrants. "We have concluded that illegal immigrants come primarily for employment."
- Imposing clear policies on benefits that distinguish between legals and illegals. "We believe that illegal aliens should be eligible for no public benefits other than those of an emergency nature, in the public health and safety interest."
- The removal of criminal aliens. "The Commission supports enhancement of the Institutional Hearing Program that permits the federal government to obtain a deportation order while criminal aliens are still serving their sentences."

When the Jordan Commission's recommendations were received by Congress, there was initial enthusiasm over their scope and potential. But once the excitement died down and the ethnic advocacy groups entered the process, those hopes were dashed. Eventually, the reforms on legal immigration were stripped from the legislation, and everything became so watered down that it was impossible to recognize Jordan's powerful clarity in the result. That was the last time the federal government attempted anything more than a piecemeal approach to immigration policy.

In early 2011, as I was finishing this book, I found myself mesmerized by the congressional debates about reducing the size of the deficit and boosting the size of the workforce. Our national debt had reached staggering levels, as had our unemployment rate, and these joint crises were stressing the nation to the breaking point. As usual, the two parties squared off on opposite sides of the issues: the Republicans demanded spending cuts and reduced taxes, and the Democrats lobbied for a greater commitment to social programs and entitlements.

As I watched the heated congressional debates, I was amazed and appalled by what I didn't hear—any acknowledgment that our immigration policies are contributing a sizeable burden to our economy. No one wanted to touch it, even though, as I have demonstrated repeatedly in this book, the numbers are convincing.

Roy Beck must have been reading my thoughts. He wrote: "When I see the anguish on the faces and in the voices of congressman after congresswoman . . . about what will be lost with each spending cut, I can't imagine why any of them would want to force more of these choices through high immigration."

Well, I can think of one reason: a complete abdication of leadership on the most significant crisis of our times. (If that's not an argument for term limits, nothing is!) We wait in vain for President Obama to give a soaring speech on immigration, as he did on race. We wait in vain for the congressional leadership from both parties to address immigration in a serious way. It has become clear that leadership will not come from the elite corridors of power in Washington but from the electorate, as they decide they're not going to tolerate the decline of their communities any longer. We have already witnessed the determination of voters on the state level. The movement is spreading.

A RALLYING PLAN OF ACTION

Immigration measures are always very controversial, but if you strip away the blind advocacy, there are many commonsense ideas that Americans can agree on.

In my own surveys on this issue, I have found a remarkable level of consensus on several key points:

- English is the language of our common principles and should be made official;
- We are obligated to enforce the laws on our books with regard to immigration;
- We should have zero tolerance for companies that hire illegal aliens;
- Jobs and services should be given preferentially to citizens of the United States;
- We should reduce quotas on legal immigrants until our unemployment crisis has ended;
- Family members eligible to immigrate on the basis of "chain migration" policies should be limited to nuclear families, not entire extended families;
- The DREAM Act should pass with a caveat that it be decoupled from family reunification;
- America should promote good governance and democracy south of our border to strengthen those societies and to make our shores less attractive to masses of illegal aliens.

These points of agreement are far from radical. They hold no bias against Hispanics or other populations. They are born of economic necessity and a future vision of a strong America. In the following chapters I will outline my plan and show how it is both possible and the right thing to do. All it requires is the leadership and the public will to act. If I were running for president, I would place at the top of my campaign promises the vow to solve the immigration problem in my first term. Then, like our eleventh president, James Polk, I might vow to forego a second term, so that my actions would remain untainted by politics. That would be an example of leadership.

Chapter 8

Step One— End Linguistic Welfare

Every immigrant who comes here should be required within five years to learn English or leave the country.

—Theodore Roosevelt

I speak three languages. My late father spoke nine. When he became a naturalized American in midcentury, it never occurred to him to demand of his new and beneficent land that whenever its government had business with him—tax forms, court proceedings, ballot boxes—that it should be required to communicate in French, his best language, rather than English, his last and relatively weakest.

—Charles Krauthammer

I speak and understand five languages and am a strong advocate for learning foreign languages. However, I expect my country to have its own language, and like many people, I am surprised and disheartened that English is not the official language of the United States. We seem to be the exception to the rule. English is the sole official language of 31 other nations. Another 20 count it as one of two or more official languages, and 1.9 billion people worldwide—one-third of all humanity—speak English. Many countries, including India and several in Africa, conduct all of their common and official business in the English language—but not the United States.

The debate about whether to make English official has gone on as long as we can remember. Every so often, members of Congress try to pass legislation to that effect to no avail. Congressional efforts to make English the official language of the United States date back to 1981, when Senator S. I. Hayakawa introduced legislation to emphasize English acquisition and reduce government multilingualism. Since that time, more than 700 members of Congress have cosponsored or voted for pending measures, including five that passed the Senate and one that passed the House of Representatives. In the 111th Congress (2010), there were nearly 140 bipartisan cosponsors of the English Language Unity Act, marking the ninth time in the past nine Congresses where an "official English" bill has garnered co-sponsorships from more than 100 representatives. Fierce lobbies oppose it, including the ACLU and Hispanic activist groups.

But even as the trend in public opinion seems firmly in the official English camp, our nation is actually growing more multilingual. On August 11, 2000, shortly before leaving office, President Clinton issued an executive order that mandated that all federal fund recipients provide multilingual services to anyone in any language that may be requested. The descriptive text read, "The Federal

Government is committed to improving the accessibility of these services to eligible LEP [limited English proficiency] persons, a goal that reinforces its equally important commitment to promoting programs and activities designed to help individuals learn English. To this end, each Federal agency shall examine the services it provides and develop and implement a system by which LEP persons can meaningfully access those services consistent with, and without unduly burdening, the fundamental mission of the agency." There was no explanation of what "unduly burdening" meant; this throwaway line had no practical definition. To date, both the federal government and the states have spent countless millions of dollars to make sure that all languages are fully heard in America.

One particularly egregious aspect of multilingual officialdom is the unfunded mandate, passed as an extension of the Voting Rights Act, that ballots be printed in every language requested. A growing number of localities are being forced to spend significant portions of their election budgets to comply with this law. Small communities with limited non-English-speaking populations are being forced to spend hundreds of thousands of dollars to produce ballots and voting manuals in Vietnamese, Chinese, Russian, Arabic, and Spanish, among a multitude of other languages. In many cases, only a handful of people actually use these materials. It's a horrendous waste of money made worse by a proliferation of lawsuits in areas where compliance is not perfect. For example, in August 2010, Cuyahoga County in Ohio was threatened with litigation by the U.S. Justice Department if it didn't provide bilingual ballots for the next election, although translating written materials, increased training, and having bilingual poll workers would cost the county close to $200,000 a year, in addition to $289,000 in transition costs. Such legal action is being duplicated across the country, thereby stressing already challenged communities. The non-English-speaking citizens bear no responsibility at all for either learning English or having voting materials privately translated.

Chaos at the Ballot Box

Nearly every state in the union requires that ballots be printed in a variety of languages, common and uncommon. Here are a few of the most extreme examples.

ALABAMA (13): Arabic, Chinese, English, Farsi, French, German, Greek, Japanese, Korean, Russian, Spanish, Thai, Vietnamese

CALIFORNIA (32): Amharic, Arabic, Armenian, Cambodian, Chinese, English, Farsi, French, German, Greek, Hebrew, Hindi, Hmong, Hungarian, Indonesian, Italian, Japanese, Korean, Laotian, Polish, Portuguese, Punjabi, Rumanian, Russian, Samoan, Serbo-Croatian, Spanish, Tagalog, Thai, Tongan, Turkish, Vietnamese

CONNECTICUT (21): Albanian, Arabic, Bosnian, Cambodian, Chinese, English, Farsi, French, German, Greek, Hebrew, Italian, Korean, Lithuanian, Polish, Portuguese, Russian, Somali, Spanish, Turkish, Vietnamese

GEORGIA (14): Arabic, Bosnian, Cambodian, Chinese, English, French, German, Japanese, Korean, Laotian, Polish, Russian, Spanish, Vietnamese

KENTUCKY (23): Albanian, Arabic, Bosnian, Cambodian, Chinese, Croatian, English, Farsi, French, German, Hindi, Japanese, Korean, Laotian, Persian, Polish, Romanian, Russian, Somali, Spanish, Thai, Turkish, Vietnamese

MASSACHUSETTS (25): Albanian, Arabic, Armenian, Cambodian, Chinese, Czech, English, Farsi, Finnish, French, German, Greek, Hebrew, Hungarian, Italian, Japanese, Korean, Laotian, Polish, Portuguese, Rumanian, Russian, Spanish, Turkish, Vietnamese

NEW YORK (12): Albanian, Arabic, Bosnian, Cambodian, Chinese, English, French, Japanese, Korean, Polish, Russian, Spanish

NORTH CAROLINA (10): Arabic, Chinese, English, French, German, Japanese, Korean, Russian, Spanish, Vietnamese

RHODE ISLAND (17): Albanian, Arabic, Cambodian, Chinese, English, French, German, Greek, Hmong, Italian, Korean, Laotian, Polish, Portuguese, Russian, Spanish, Vietnamese

Year after year, the burden becomes only greater as more languages are added to the official column.

THE BENEFITS OF OFFICIAL ENGLISH

The idea of an official national language is not strange or unusual or offensive. Ninety-two percent of the world's nations have one. Some people who oppose making English the official language point out that there is no mention of it in the Constitution. But there's a good reason for that. The issue was never discussed at the Constitutional Convention. Because more than 90 percent of the non-slave population was of British ancestry, and even the former Dutch colonies had been under English rule for more than a century, the topic was not controversial enough even to be debated. Most people spoke English. Period.

What are the benefits of making English official? First and foremost, it would be a powerful declaration to promote unity. People in the United States speak more than 322 languages, and English should stand at the heart of them all, bringing us together. Instead, the number of Americans who don't speak English at all has quadrupled in the past 30 years. Once again, Theodore Roosevelt had it right when he declared in 1907, "Let us say to the immigrant not that we hope he will learn English, but that he has got to learn it. Let the immigrant who does not learn it go back. He has got to consider the interest of the United States or he should not stay here. He must be made to see that his opportunities in this country depend upon his knowing English and observing American standards. The employer cannot be permitted to regard him only as an industrial asset." In other words, language is the glue that holds people of common mind together—and being of common mind is a high value for Americans.

Supporting native languages other than English, especially in official situations such as courtrooms, classrooms, and driver's license bureaus, actually makes it more difficult for immigrants to thrive. Studies repeatedly show that immigrants do more poorly when they receive native language support instead of being forced to learn *our* native language. Immigrants will benefit from the elevation of English to official status. Instead of the mixed message government sends by making it possible to file tax returns, vote, become U.S. citizens, and receive a host of other services in a variety of languages, immigrants will understand that they must know English to participate fully in the process of government.

It's a plain fact that "linguistic welfare" dooms many immigrants to lives of low-skilled, low-paying jobs. You really can't make it in America without English proficiency. Studies show that an immigrant's income rises about 30 percent when he or she learns English. The realization of the American dream relies on a degree of assimilation. We say we're being benevolent by letting people speak their native tongue, but in reality we're condemning them to a subpar lifestyle. If the guy on the construction site doesn't speak English, he's always going to be hauling dirt. It's just a fact.

In studies by the National Adult Literacy Survey, the average employed immigrant who spoke English very well earned $40,741, more than double the $16,345 earned by the immigrant who did not speak English at all. The increasing scale of English proficiency and earnings was recorded at every education level from less than high school to master's degree and beyond. Immigrants with a low degree of English proficiency earned one-half of what those with a medium degree of proficiency earned and less than one-third of highly English-proficient immigrants.

According to the U.S. Department of Labor, immigrants who speak English "not well" or "not at all" have median weekly earnings approximately 57 percent of those of U.S.-born workers. The weekly earnings of immigrants who speak another language at home but speak English "very well" or "well" are nearly 90 percent of those of U.S.-born workers. Immigrants who speak English at home are best off, with median weekly earnings 20 percent higher than U.S.-born workers.

The U.S. Department of Education found that those with limited English proficiency are less likely to be employed, are less likely to be employed continuously, tend to work in the least desirable sectors, and earn less than those who speak English. Annual earnings by non-English-proficient adults were approximately half of the total population surveyed.

The Tomas Rivera Policy Institute, a Latino think tank, found that "far and away, the most commonly cited obstacle to gaining college knowledge was the language barrier." While 96 percent of the Latino parents surveyed in the nation's three largest cities expected their children to go to college, nearly two-thirds missed at least half the questions on a "mini-test of college knowledge"—a result judged to be related to language skills.

Making English the official language is also a practical matter. The duplication of official services costs taxpayers hundreds of millions of dollars a year. These include the costs of hiring bilingual teachers, printing bilingual textbooks, translating every government Web site into multiple languages, and requiring every agency and department throughout the entire United States to hire translators and/or print materials to ensure that any person, speaking any language, can receive government services in his or her language of choice. With the Clinton bill, these mandates were extended to companies doing business with the federal government or receiving benefits from the federal government, such as contractors, schools, hospitals, churches, and nonprofit organizations.

In virtually very place where a non-English-speaking person might require services, they must be provided in his or her native tongue.

Consider the Department of Motor Vehicles, one agency severely burdened by the need to operate in multiple official languages. Not only is DMV multilingualism prohibitively expensive but also it is increasingly being cited as a safety issue. Road signs across the land are printed in English, and the failure to understand and follow signs has led to accidents and fatalities. To date, the evidence is anecdotal, but it stands to reason that drivers who are unable to read traffic signs (and unable to read and understand our motor vehicle laws) are liable to have many more accidents.

Offical English for Driver's Licenses Model Legislation

STATE OF [state name]

BE IT ENACTED BY THE PEOPLE OF THE STATE OF [state name]:

SECTION 1. A new section of law to be codified in the [state name] Statutes as Section [—] of Title [—], read as follows:

This act shall be known and may be cited as the Highway Safety Act.

SECTION 2. A new section of law to be codified in the [state name] Statutes as Section [—] of Title [—], read as follows:

A. All examinations of applicants for a commercial vehicle operator's license, whether written or otherwise, shall be conducted exclusively in the English language.

B. State agency shall neither supply nor permit the use of interpreters in connection with conducting examinations of applicants.

C. Applicants must be able to read and speak the English language sufficiently to converse with the general public, understand highway traffic signs and signals in the English language, respond to official inquiries, and make entries on reports and records.

SECTION 3. This Act shall become effective [month day], 20__

Congress may be chronically bogged down when it comes to passing this obvious measure of national unity, but the people have spoken time and again about their desire to make English official. Most recently, a 2010 survey by Rasmussen Reports found that 84 percent of Americans believed English should be the official language of the United States. Seventy-five percent also believed that companies should be allowed to require their employees to speak English on the job. In the survey, only 12 percent of voters believed that requiring employees to speak English is a form of racism or bigotry.

The survey noted that during the 2008 presidential campaign, then-Senator Obama said that it was more important for American children to learn to speak Spanish than it was for new immigrants to learn to speak English. In the poll, 83 percent of voters disagreed, saying a higher priority should be placed on encouraging immigrants to speak English as their primary language.

The States Fight Back!
Official English Laws on the Books in 31 States

Alabama (1990)	Massachusetts (1975)
Alaska (1998)	Mississippi (1987)
Arizona (2006)	Missouri (1998, 2008)
Arkansas (1987)	Montana (1995)
California (1986)	Nebraska (1920)
Colorado (1988)	New Hampshire (1995)
Florida (1988)	North Carolina (1987)
Georgia (1986, 1996)	North Dakota (1987)
Hawaii (1978)	Oklahoma (2010)
Idaho (2007)	South Carolina (1987)
Illinois (1969)	South Dakota (1995)
Indiana (1984)	Tennessee (1984)
Iowa (2002)	Utah (2000)
Kansas (2007)	Virginia (1981, 1996)
Kentucky (1984)	Wyoming (1996)
Louisiana (1812)	

Myth and reality

Let's put to rest some of the biggest myths about making English the official language.

Myth: Official English means English only

Official English is a limitation only on government. It does not affect the languages spoken in private businesses, religious services, or private conversations. In short, English is the official language for business conducted at the federal, state and local levels.

Myth: Official English would deny due process to citizens.

The ACLU believes that English-only laws can violate the U.S. Constitution's protection of due process (especially in courts where no translation service would be offered) and equal protection (for example, English-only ballots being used where bilingual ones were available in the past). However, everyone agrees that English-only laws would have exceptions for public safety and legal necessities. The justice system would continue to provide language assistance to criminal defendants and victims of crime, and the 911 emergency system would remain accessible to all. Government employees would continue to provide informal assistance and directions in any language they felt appropriate. These and other commonsense exceptions would be built into any official English bill.

Myth: Official English would bar nonnative celebrations such as St. Patrick's Day, Cinco de Mayo, and Oktoberfest.

Official English refers solely to business conducted by government entities, with specific exemptions for mottoes, holiday celebrations, and the like. Not only would nonnative holidays continue to be celebrated after the enactment

123

of official English but also these special days would likely be joined by other cultural festivities taught to Americans by newcomers speaking a shared language—English.

MYTH: OFFICIAL ENGLISH WOULD PROHIBIT THE TEACHING OF FOREIGN LANGUAGES IN SCHOOLS.

Since it deals with only government entities, publications, and documents, the enactment of official English would not affect the teaching of foreign languages. Indeed, proficiency in multiple languages opens more doors and raises incomes even higher than proficiency in a single native language.

MYTH: OFFICIAL ENGLISH WOULD ACTUALLY HAMPER THE EFFORTS OF NEW IMMIGRANTS TO LEARN ENGLISH BY REDUCING ESL FUNDING.

According to ProEnglish, an organization that supports official English, reliable research shows that ESL programs fail to teach students the English language and literacy they need for school success. On the organization's Web site it declares: "Segregation by language and ethnicity does not lead to higher academic performance, does not raise students' self-esteem, results in social isolation and may contribute to high drop-out rates. Delaying the learning of English, the language of school and community life, holds back student achievement. Graduating from high school without fluency and literacy in English deprives students of opportunity in an English-speaking country."

MYTH: IMMIGRANTS RESIST LEARNING ENGLISH.

According to a poll by Zogby International, 81 percent of first- and second-generation Americans favor making English the official language of the United States. Majority support for official English was recorded among every sub-group, including age, gender, race, and political affiliation.

English proficiency rates among immigrants vary widely by ancestry. More than 80 percent of the immigrants from several ancestry groups speak English "very well," including Egyptians (90.4 percent), Lebanese (89.5), Pakistanis (87.7), Romanians (86.5), Iranians (86.1), Thais (83.0), and Argentineans (81.6). Other ancestry groups lag far behind the overall average of 71.4 percent English proficient, including Cambodians (65.7), Vietnamese (64.4), Hondurans (53.5), Guatemalans (52.8), and Mexicans (49.9).

OFFICIAL ENGLISH: A PLATFORM

I propose that we take three basic actions to achieve linguistic unity.

ACTION 1: DECLARE ENGLISH THE OFFICIAL LANGUAGE.

In early 2011, Representative Steve King of Iowa and 60 other members of the House of Representatives launched the latest effort to make English the official language of the United States. The English Language Unity Act of 2011 would reduce government multilingualism and focus government agencies on promoting English acquisition. It would require the U.S. government to conduct most official business in English. Specifically, the bill would limit routine government operations to English while giving government agencies common-sense exceptions to protect public health and safety and national security and to provide for the needs of commerce and the criminal justice system.

The bill, which is expected to enjoy the most congressional support in nearly a decade, is still in committee and is being prepared for a full vote of the House before it is sent on to the Senate for further debate and final confirmation.

ACTION 2: INSTITUTE ENGLISH IMMERSION PROGRAMS.

While experts agree that ESL programs have been largely a failure, there is wide support for English immersion programs, called structured English immersion (SEI). In these programs, students spend one full school year (or longer, if necessary) studying the English language: learning to speak, read, and write and to master the vocabulary they need to learn school subjects taught in English. As soon as students are skilled in English, they join their classmates in regular classrooms where all teaching is in English. In both California and Arizona, state test reports show students learning English in an average of two years and achieving passing scores on reading and math tests as well. These results are not unusual.

Research comparing students in bilingual programs with students in SEI has reported far better results in the SEI classes. A Lexington Institute study published in 2008 found that some of the highest-performing students in California public schools are children who started kindergarten with little or no English. In June 2009, the state of Massachusetts reported that in 17 of the 42 Boston high schools, the valedictorian of the graduating class was a student who had come from another country within the past few years, without any knowledge of English. Thanks to SEI programs, these students excelled.

ACTION 3: SUPPORT ON-THE-JOB RETRAINING.

For decades, the federal government's Equal Employment Opportunity Commission has targeted employers that adopt English-language workplace rules. Although the courts have repeatedly affirmed that employers have the right to establish English-language policies, the EEOC disputes these rulings and continues to harass employers, even when the courts say it has no authority to do so. According to the organization ProEnglish, "The EEOC appears to have implemented a strategy of trying to gain settlements from small businesses which do not have the resources to defend themselves in court. These settlements could then be used to create a legal precedent that contradicts earlier federal-court rulings."

One recent example is RD's, a family-owned drive-through restaurant in rural Arizona. This small business was targeted by the EEOC with a charge that it discriminated against employees on the basis of national origin by implementing an English-language workplace policy. Navajo-speaking bilingual employees had been using the Navajo language to harass and demean fellow employees and customers. This is perhaps an extreme example, but it makes the case that where employers are denied the right to establish workplace language policies, chaos ensues.

I believe that passing legislation to make English our nation's official language, along with supportive measures that favor English immersion and on-the-job training, would have an immediate cathartic effect on our nation.

In 1828, when Noah Webster published the first *American Dictionary of the English Language*, he did so with a fierce sense of national pride. His goal was to celebrate the uniqueness of America and to bring its citizens together through a common language that was distinct from all others—even from the style of English spoken by the British. The same spirit is true today. The only way we can unify the most diverse nation in the world is through a common language.

Chapter 9

Step Two—Enforce the Laws on the Books

Credibility in immigration policy can be summed up in one sentence: Those who should get in, get in; those who should be kept out, are kept out; and those who should not be here will be required to leave.

—the late Congresswoman Barbara Jordan, when she was chair of the U.S. Commission on Immigration Reform

One of the most discouraging aspects of immigration control has been a consistent lack of commitment about enforcing laws already on the books. This situation has grown much worse under the Obama administration's soft enforcement policies. In early 2011, Obama announced the creation of a new Employment Compliance Inspection Center, intended to increase audits on employers suspected of hiring illegals. On the face of it, this compassionate approach would seem to be an effective, bulletless way to control illegal immigration. However, we're kidding ourselves if we think a few fines here and there will bring down a tenacious system of illegality. Simply fining companies and forcing them to fire illegals still leaves the illegals on the loose, free to find jobs elsewhere, and the vicious cycle starts again.

A recent report by the Pew Hispanic Center showed that the number of U.S. jobs held by illegal foreign workers has remained steady in recent years at about eight million, proving that enforcement policies just shuffle the illegal labor pool rather than eliminating it.

One reason may be that the Obama administration has quietly changed the way enforcement is practiced. On July 1, 2009, U.S. Immigration and Customs Enforcement announced a policy change from that of the Bush administration. Now, instead of issuing criminal search warrants against employers suspected of hiring illegals and instead of bursting into workplaces unannounced, the agency would follow the procedure of issuing companies a notice of the intent to audit, thus giving everyone plenty of time to work it out and the illegals plenty of time to disappear. If it didn't seem insane, I'd say the Obama administration didn't want to deal with illegals' acting against America's national interest.

Mark Krikorian testified before the Judiciary Subcommittee on Immigration Policy and Enforcement in January 2011: "As part of the current administration's

April 2009 Worksite Enforcement Strategy, real worksite enforcement has declined significantly, with administrative arrests down by more than half compared with 2008, criminal arrests down by more than half, likewise with indictments and convictions. What have increased in this area are audits of employee I-9 forms and the number and total dollar amount of fines against employers. Such audits and fines are by no means a bad thing, as far as they go. But they don't go very far.

"By limiting worksite enforcement to the personnel office, the current strategy foregoes the benefits of full-spectrum enforcement that includes both audits and raids, both fines and arrests, focused on both the employers and the employees. A colleague observed to me yesterday that the current ICE focus on audits is as effective as the FBI doing gang suppression by just giving talks at high schools, without actually arresting any gang members."

It's simply a myth that when the feds target a workplace for hiring illegals, the illegals end up being deported. Instead, they're free to work again. In effect, we could discover the same illegal alien over and over and over again. It's like trying to hold water in a sieve.

Chipotle, a national chain of Mexican restaurants, is a perfect case study. Chipotle had been under observation by the feds for some time on the basis of evidence that the chain employed many thousands of illegals. When the federal government announced its intention to audit Chipotles in Minnesota, what was the result? The company began firing people, and others just quit and disappeared. While the threat of an audit allowed hundreds of jobs to be filled by American workers, it stopped short of true enforcement because the illegals are still in the communities and are just seeking jobs elsewhere.

Even more disturbing, Department of Homeland Security Secretary Janet Napolitano admitted to Congress in early 2011 that her agency had granted deferred action to 900 illegal aliens in 2010—not counting an unannounced number that were deferred for "humanitarian" reasons. The decision to grant deferments is made at the sole discretion of Napolitano and is not subject to congressional or judicial review. Why were these deferments made? We don't really know, although we know that the majority were people who had overstayed their visas. Nine hundred may not seem like a very large number in the scheme of things, but Napolitano's action is suspect on the basis of her often-asserted support for the administration's pro-amnesty position.

What the Obama administration is *not* committed to, in my opinion, is the rule of law when it comes to immigration. In late 2010, the administration launched a plan to prevent illegals caught in traffic stops from being deported. The reasoning was that if police had the authority to hold traffic violators on immigration grounds, they would be prone to stop "innocent" drivers for the sole purpose of checking their status. This fear seems completely without substance. Where is the documented evidence that police officers would be likely to behave this way? Even if they did, what harm would be done? On numerous occasions I have been stopped at airports, both here and abroad, for looking Middle Eastern. It does not bother me at all because in the end my children's civil right to have their father come home in one piece should take precedence over being politically correct. While I believe that we must never tolerate discrimination based on the color of our skin, I fail to see how a request for identification amounts to harassment. I can only imagine how frustrating plans like this are to law enforcement officers, who are charged with upholding the law. It seems counterproductive to the spirit of law enforcement. What our nation needs is tougher enforcement, not a wishy-washy system.

Do immigration crackdowns work? Enforcement in the form of raids may offend the sensibilities of some people, but they can be effective. The Smithfield pork plant in Tar Heel, North Carolina, is a case in point. The largest hog-processing facility in the world, it slaughters up to 32,000 hogs a day, slices them into a variety of cuts, and sends them to market. According to the Center for Immigration Studies, which monitored the case, in January 2007 Immigration and Customs Enforcement agents raided the plant in a crackdown on illegal immigrants who were said to be employed at very low wages. Hundreds were arrested at the plant and at their homes in surrounding areas and scheduled for deportation. Other illegal workers, fearing they might be detained, left the plant on their own. The action resulted in the transfer of more than 1,500 jobs from illegal aliens to American blacks. The black American share of the workforce climbed from just 20 percent before the raids to 60 percent afterward.

One clear benefit of immigration crackdowns is that they not only open up jobs but also raise wages for American workers. At the Smithfield plant, only after the raid took place were attempts to unionize in order to bargain for better wages successful.

In another pre-Obama case, 1,300 illegal workers were arrested at six meatpacking plants owned by Swift & Co. in the largest-ever worksite enforcement action. All the plants resumed production the same day, and all were back to full production within five months, despite the fact that nearly one-quarter of the total workforce had been illegal aliens. Most importantly, at the four facilities where information was available, wages and bonuses rose on average 8 percent after the departure of the illegal workers.

When companies argue that illegal immigrants are necessary to do jobs American workers won't do, what they really mean is that companies can't treat American workers with the same disregard. Americans won't stand for subpar wages or unsafe workplace conditions. So, yes, there is more pressure on companies such as Smithfield in the wake of immigration raids to clean up their workplaces and start offering competitive wages. This can only be a good thing. By the way, although meatpacking is one of the most grueling and dirtiest jobs there is, these plants had no trouble at all replacing illegals with American workers.

In his congressional testimony in January 2011, Krikorian urged members to support full-scale workplace enforcement. "While the goal of worksite enforcement is not to try to actually arrest and deport every illegal worker, every illegal worker does need to know that he could be arrested at any time," Krikorian insisted. "Likewise, the goal is not to fine or arrest every employer of illegal aliens, but rather to ensure that employers are aware that there's a realistic chance of that happening to them. . . . In the absence of across-the-board enforcement, neither illegal workers nor their employers have much to fear from law enforcement; on the contrary, they get the hint that what they're doing isn't really all that illegal after all. Under such conditions, the decline we saw in the illegal population as a result of enhanced enforcement (before the recession began) will not take place. In fact, if and when the job market significantly improves, today's constrained and limited approach to worksite enforcement virtually ensures that the illegal population will start growing again."

ATTRITION THROUGH ENFORCEMENT

Attrition through enforcement is a simple and logical idea: make living illegally in the United States so difficult that people won't want to do it. How is this accomplished? *By rigorous enforcement of the laws on the books.* According to proponents of this policy, it can be effective and also affordable—and is a substitute for the unworkable, inhuman, draconian idea of mass deportation. Beck says, "There is no need for taxpayers to watch the government spend billions of their dollars to round up and deport illegal aliens; they will buy their own bus or plane tickets back home if they can no longer earn a living here." And we must make "home" an attractive option for those illegal aliens that lose their jobs through tough enforcement.

At a time when our economy seems to have entered a structural evolution to low growth, attrition through enforcement can create new jobs for blacks, teens, the elderly, and low-income whites. For example, if it was practiced at restaurants, hotels, motels, office buildings, construction sites, and other places illegals work, we could potentially create eight million new jobs at higher wages.

As it stands now, there isn't much incentive for illegals to leave on their own. Our government's ongoing flirtation with amnesty, its tolerance for birthright citizenship, and its lackluster enforcement measures make it, frankly, no big deal to be illegal here. But what would happen if the atmosphere were to become far less tolerant, and the illegal aliens had a chance of a new beginning in their home countries?

In 2010, Arizona pioneered a strict brand of attrition-through-enforcement legislation, whose intent was to discourage and deter the unlawful entry and presence of aliens and economic activity by persons unlawfully living in the United States. The law, which proponents and critics alike said was the broadest and most severe immigration measure in generations, would make the failure to carry immigration documents a crime and would give the police broad power to detain anyone suspected of being in the country illegally.

Opponents considered it an open invitation for harassment and discrimination against Hispanics regardless of their citizenship status. Critics were immediately concerned about racial profiling and said that all Hispanics would bear the burden of proof. Arizona began to take an immediate economic hit from organizations that canceled plans to hold events in the state, as well as individuals who refused to visit or send their children to colleges there. Protest rallies were held across the country. The Justice Department immediately filed suit against Arizona by claiming that the law interfered with federal immigration responsibilities. However, Governor Jan Brewer stated that Arizona was simply responding to the overwhelming economic costs of being a border state. A Rasmussen poll taken shortly after the law was passed found that 60 percent of all Americans supported it and were also in favor of similar laws in their own states.

Many people felt that Arizona had been forced to act because Congress just wasn't getting the job done. Bill after bill designed to strengthen enforcement and deal with the illegal alien problem was regularly defeated. Inaction was the name of the game in Washington.

In my opinion, the Arizona law, while strict, was entirely reasonable. Why must we tiptoe around the feelings of people who flaunt our laws by coming here illegally or who support those who do? Being asked to show identification papers is a minor inconvenience. The only reason an individual would have cause to fear doing so would be if he or she could not pass muster.

Most of the problem would be solved by the issuance of national ID cards. I simply do not understand why there is such strong objection to this. According to the ACLU and others, the issuance of national ID cards would set in motion a Big Brother–style level of snooping that would interfere with our rights to privacy. But that's ridiculous. We already have passports. We have driver's licenses. We have Social Security numbers. What are we afraid of?

136

One strategy of attrition through enforcement is to limit benefits to illegals. In 1994, California voters passed Proposition 187 (also known as SOS—Save Our State). In a dramatic declaration, the proposition read: "The People of California find and declare as follows: That they have suffered and are suffering economic hardship caused by the presence of illegal aliens in this state. That they have suffered and are suffering personal injury and damage caused by the criminal conduct of illegal aliens in this state. That they have a right to the protection of their government from any person or persons entering this country unlawfully." The measure would have created a state-run citizenship-screening system in order to prohibit illegal immigrants from using health care, public education, and other social services. The proposed law, which was extremely popular with embattled Californians, was initially passed by the voters through referendum in November 1994 but later was found to be unconstitutional by a federal court, with appeals against the judgment being halted by Governor Gray Davis in 1999. Davis was later recalled, in large part by residents unhappy with his position on Proposition 187.

Proposition 187 was a sign that the will of the people was moving toward harsher enforcement. However, there were logistical problems that would have become apparent soon enough. As one law enforcement agent put it, it was "closer to the bull's tail than the bull's-eye." It would have established an unwieldy bureaucracy that might have overwhelmed any efforts toward true reform and thus created a large underclass-in-hiding. In the process, it would have taken attention off legitimate enforcement and border control efforts.

Just about every serious border control measure has foundered in Congress. The most recent and promising was the SAVE Act of 2007, which called for increasing border patrol agents by 8,000; the use of new technology and fencing to secure the border; expansion of specialized enforcement programs, such as the "Tunnel Task Force"; and strengthening enforcement of employer hiring laws. SAVE never became law.

Another piece of legislation was the CLEAR Act, designed to clarify state and local officers' authority to detain illegal aliens. It also required the federal government to respond to state and local requests to pick up and remove illegals.

The CLEAR Act promised to increase State Criminal Alien Assistance Funds for communities that worked with federal agencies to enforce immigration laws, improved information sharing between federal agencies and local communities, and increased federal enforcement resources and standards for removing illegal aliens quickly. It, too, failed to become law.

In April 2010, Senators John McCain and John Kyl, both Republicans from Arizona, introduced a 10-point border security plan that they said would dramatically improve Arizona's effort to fight illegal immigration and solve problems of drug-related violence along the border. Their plan was an effort to speak to the Obama administration's assertion that border security could not happen independently of a comprehensive immigration plan. Not true, said McCain: "The lesson is clear: First we have to secure the border. If you want to enact some other reforms, how can that be effective when you have a porous border? So we have to secure the border first." In fact, according to a former official at DHS, the U.S. government has failed to develop good measures for fixing goals and determining progress towards border security.

To date, the McCain/Kyl plan has not gained a foothold, and that's a shame because I believe it is thoughtful and complete. Ask any border enforcement agent to review it and you'll get an affirmative response. The plan calls for the following actions:

1. The immediate deployment of 3,000 National Guard Troops along the Arizona-Mexico border, along with appropriate surveillance platforms, which shall remain in place until the governor of Arizona certifies, after consulting with state, local, and tribal law enforcement, that the federal government has achieved operational control of the border. Permanently add 3,000 Custom and Border Protection Agents to the Arizona-Mexico border by 2015.

2. Fully fund and support Operation Streamline in Arizona's two border patrol sectors to, at a minimum, ensure that repeat illegal border crossers go to jail for 15–60 days. Where Operation Streamline has been implemented, the number of illegal crossings has decreased significantly.

Require the Obama administration to complete a required report detailing the justice and enforcement resources needed to fully fund this program. Fully reimburse localities for any related detention costs.

3. Provide $100 million, an increase of $40 million, for Operation Stonegarden, a program that provides grants and reimbursement to Arizona's border law enforcement for additional personnel, overtime, travel, and other related costs related to illegal immigration and drug smuggling along the border.

4. Offer hardship duty pay to border patrol agents assigned to rural high-trafficked areas, such as the CBP Willcox and Douglas stations in the Tucson sector.

5. Complete the 700 miles of fencing along the border with Mexico and construct double- and triple-layer fencing at appropriate locations along the Arizona-Mexico border.

6. Substantially increase the 25 mobile surveillance systems and three Predator B unmanned aerial vehicles (UAVs) in place today along the Arizona-Mexico border and ensure that the border patrol has the resources necessary to operate the UAVs 24 hours a day, seven days a week. Send additional fixed-wing aircraft and helicopters to the Arizona-Mexico border.

7. Increase funding for vital radio communications and interoperability between CBP and state, local, and tribal law enforcement to assist in apprehensions along the border.

8. Provide funding for additional border patrol stations in the Tucson sector and explore the possibility of an additional border patrol sector for Arizona. Create six additional permanent Border Patrol Forward Operating Bases, and provide funding to upgrade the existing bases to include modular buildings, electricity, and potable water. Complete construction of the planned permanent checkpoint in Arizona. Deploy additional temporary roving checkpoints and increase horse patrols throughout the Tucson sector.

9. Require the federal government to fully reimburse state and local governments for the costs of incarcerating criminal aliens. Start by at least funding the State Criminal Alien Assistance Program (SCAAP) at its authorized level of $950 million.

10. Place one full-time federal magistrate in Cochise County and provide full funding for and authorization of the Southwest Border Prosecution Initiative to reimburse state, county, tribal, and municipal governments for costs associated with the prosecution and pretrial detention of federally initiated criminal cases declined by local offices of the U.S. Attorneys.

A year has passed as of this writing, and McCain says he's ready to present the plan again. It's scandalous that commonsense enforcement measures such as this one continue to gather dust in the halls of Congress. The way Congress drags its feet on every tough piece of immigration legislation is quite discouraging, especially since the population at large is overwhelmingly in favor of tougher measures. For example:

- > 78 percent of American voters support the creation of a tamper-proof ID card system to determine instantly whether a job applicant is legally entitled to work inside the United States and to hold those employers who hire illegal workers accountable.

- > 75 percent of American voters favor prohibiting states from issuing driver's licenses to illegal immigrants.

- > 77 percent of American voters favor repealing local sanctuary laws that protect illegal immigrants by requiring local and state police to detain illegal immigrants when they are arrested or stopped for other crimes, whether these crimes are felonies or misdemeanors, and to hold them for deportation.

- > 68 percent of American voters support enacting a new immigration policy of zero tolerance toward illegal immigrants, where any illegal immigrant in the United States would be deported to his or her country of citizenship.

What are we waiting for?

The question is, What are the methods of enforcement that could actually work right now that are, in fact, already on the books? Here are some starting points.

Fix and enforce E-Verify

E-Verify is an Internet-based system that allows businesses to determine the eligibility of their employees to work in the United States. E-Verify is fast, free, and easy to use, and it's the best way employers can ensure a legal workforce. While the system is mandatory for federal agencies, it is largely voluntary for private employers. Many people feel that should change. There is a growing sense that E-Verify can work only if it is applied completely and consistently, and hundreds of state legislators across the country are trying to put their unemployed residents back to work by passing mandatory E-Verify laws. Who could object? The strongest pushback has come from business lobbyists and the Chamber of Commerce, who labor under the unfounded assumption that crackdowns of illegal aliens would hurt business. These groups have formed a strange alliance with the ACLU, which falsely states that E-Verify is a discriminatory program.

How accurate is E-Verify? According to U.S. Citizenship and Immigration Services, which manages E-Verify within the Department of Homeland Security, the current accuracy rate of E-Verify is better than 99.5 percent:

- \> 97.4 percent of employees are automatically confirmed as authorized to work either instantly or within 24 hours, thus requiring no employee or employer action.
- \> 2.6 percent of employees receive initial system mismatches. Of these, 0.03 percent of employees need to contact the Social Security

Administration or USCIS to correct mistakes on their records. The remaining 2.3 percent of employees are found not to be work authorized and are terminated by their employers. (Most of these simply fail to show up for work again rather than waiting to be fired.) These numbers correspond closely to an estimate by the Pew Hispanic Center that illegal aliens hold 4.9 percent of U.S. jobs.

According to Roy Beck, really enforcing E-Verify could pay big dividends and make it a "small patch of immigration policy ground that could result in millions of unemployed Americans and immigrants getting back to work." Beck points out that "those who would most benefit from this common-ground effort are among the weakest members of our society, particularly less-educated younger adults, who are competing most directly with non-agricultural illegal workers."

The Center for Immigration Studies has written extensively about the benefits of E-Verify, including:

- Protection of jobs for authorized U.S. workers, who will spend and invest their wages in the local community rather than transferring a large portion to foreign countries.
- Reduction of verification-related discrimination and the protection of civil liberties and employee privacy.
- Protection for human resource professionals and hiring managers who may otherwise be pressured by employers to hire illegal aliens and later be charged with serious offenses while their employers go free.
- Protecting employers using E-Verify, who cannot be charged with a verification violation should an employee present the employer with documents that reasonably appear to be genuine and related to the employee presenting them.
- Elimination of any pretense that an identity thief didn't knowingly use another person's identity because, in the case of total identity theft, the

identity thief deliberately uses the victim's exact name in place of his or her own name.

Opponents of E-Verify have been unable to find a single instance in which an employer relying on an erroneous E-Verify result terminated a U.S. citizen or a legal resident.

The main concern expressed by people who challenge E-Verify is that it is open to abuse through identity theft. There is no question that the identity theft loophole exists. A certain number of applicants have sailed through the verification process because they were using stolen names and Social Security numbers. However, the Department of Homeland Security has taken a significant step toward closing this loophole by including photos from immigration documents in the system so an employer verifying a noncitizen employee will be able to compare the photo on the immigration document presented by the employee with the photo that comes up on his or her computer screen during the verification process.

The Social Security Administration could close the loophole almost entirely if it would simply notify workers with more than one employer making contributions to their Social Security account numbers and ask them to report whether they were not actually working for each of those employers. However, inexplicably, SSA has a policy of not informing the victims of identity theft—which brings us to the importance of REAL ID.

Implement REAL ID

On May 11, 2005, President George W. Bush signed into law the Emergency Supplemental Appropriation for Defense, the Global War on Terror, and Tsunami Relief, 2005, which included the REAL ID Act. This act heightened standards for driver's licenses and made state databases nationally compatible. It was considered a no-brainer, as most people use driver's licenses as their primary means of identification. REAL ID was initiated as a recommendation by the 9/11 Commission, after discovering that the 19 hijackers had acquired

30 different state-issued IDs among them. The commission felt it was essential to ensure that people were who they said they were. REAL ID requires that those applying for a driver's license present vital records such as a birth certificate, proof of Social Security number, and proof of legal residence. Databases would be digitalized to make it easy for officials to cross check by state or nationally, with paper copies and microfiche maintained for a minimum of seven years. Once all of these conditions are met and the license is issued, a branding star would be affixed to the upper right-hand corner of the license to show that it meets REAL ID guidelines.

Unfortunately, the states have been slow to comply, and some have resisted compliance or created their own alternative systems. By January 2011, only 11 states were fully compliant, with 10 others partially complaint. Compliance deadlines continued to be extended, and on March 4, 2011, Napolitano extended them once again from May 2011 to January 2013.

However, states are beginning to come around at a faster pace after finding it anti-productive to resist. States without REAL ID found themselves overwhelmed by illegal alien applications at their DMVs. An example of this was my home state of Maryland. Maryland was initially opposed to REAL ID implementation because it feared the process would be too costly and would somehow infringe on citizen rights. But in 2008, Governor Martin O'Malley pushed for the language to be added to legislation, and REAL ID was passed, with much grumbling and continued resistance. Still, by 2008, Maryland was 100 percent compliant, and you don't hear complaints anymore. On the very first day of implementation, 8,000 application interviews were canceled. It is not a stretch to assume that these were 8,000 individuals whose IDs could not withstand scrutiny.

In total, of the 50 U.S. states and six territories, 44 (41 states and three territories) of them have given DHS the green light that they are on board and working toward REAL ID compliance. Of the remaining nine states and three territories, three of those states have laws banning the state from compliance, yet two of them are meeting REAL ID standards without using the REAL ID name.

Sadly, in spite of the program's proven advantages and its moderate cost, the passionate naysayers are out in force to rewrite the regulation or, worse, start from scratch. These groups include the American Association of Motor Vehicle Administrations (AAMVA), the National Governors Association, and the National Conference of State Legislatures. Basically, these groups want to water down the provision, such as weakening the background documentation required, further lengthening the period for compliance, and (inexplicably) removing the branding star from licenses.

I believe strongly that we must hold firm on the REAL ID standards as they were written and the states must speed up their compliance. Leadership is required on the federal and state levels to show how well the program works in those states that comply.

Privatize wisely

Anger and frustration with our current enforcement models are absolutely warranted. The federal government does not have the resources or ability to achieve more than scattershot victories. If we were to privatize one or more enforcement arms of immigration, it would stiffen accountability and produce revenue while getting the job done. I understand that there's a knee-jerk aversion to privatization, based on the mental image many people have of pickup trucks full of vigilante-style outliers pointing their guns and rounding up illegal aliens. You might see that in the movies, but the private enforcement companies I envision are professional investigative and technological organizations, perhaps public entities traded on the stock exchange, and their monetary value would be measured by their success. Systematically reported apprehension rates and deterrence data would give the American public better information to decide which company to invest in. For example, an affiliate of Boeing would be given the task of monitoring the California-Mexico border to ensure no illegal entries. A Lockheed affiliate would be asked to control the flow of illegal immigration along the Texas-Mexico border. A Raytheon spin-off would manage the Arizona-Mexico border. The American public would be given a Web site to visit in order to track the success of these newly created companies that trade on the NYSE in apprehending illegal immigrants. Tying the value of these companies' stock to the national interest of America in apprehending illegal immigrants and allowing the American public to monitor their progress would ensure that companies assigned to this task perform the job within the strict confines of our laws and create wealth for their shareholders.

Another option is one currently being worked on at the University of Arizona, which has emerged as an innovative center to address technological security opportunities. The university has partnered with the Department of Homeland Security and private industry to create the Border Security and Technology Commercialization Center (BSTCC). The center will help private companies identify how their products can be applied to border security, trade, and immigration. Research at BSTCC will focus on new technologies such as surveillance screening, data fusion, and situational awareness using sensors, unmanned aerial vehicles, and other technologies. The center also will provide research on population dynamics; immigration administration and enforcement; operational analysis, control, and communications; immigration policy; civic integration and citizenship; border risk management; and international governance.

Educational programs will include training programs to develop science, technology, and management solutions to prepare the next generation of border security professionals while further enhancing the skills of personnel currently in the field. The center also will provide tools and practices that can be rapidly deployed to end users.

BSTCC is a promising collaboration between education, government, and private industry that just might work. I like the long-range aspects of the program, which have the effect of creating a culture of security consciousness born of real solutions from the best efforts of capitalism.

Simplify!

Finally, I have to say something about the confusion and duplication rampant in national security and immigration enforcement programs. Why are there two or three different programs devoted to establishing one database? Why does each new administration further muddy the waters with its own signature effort, even when it duplicates others and leaves us swimming in a sea of acronyms? Why are states given so much leeway to devise their own standards when this is clearly a national problem? Our commitment to immigration reform and enforcement is contingent on our ability to make sense of our laws so they can be effectively enforced.

Chapter 10

Step Three—A Five-Year Immigration Moratorium

The first priority of our government needs to be the interests of American citizens—both native born and naturalized—not legal immigrant workers. And the 25 million American citizens out of work are not only pushed out by illegal aliens, but also by certain legal immigrants.

—Virgil Goode

With job stagnation expected to last for years, what better time than now to resurrect the conversation about an immigration moratorium? From a pure dollars-and-cents perspective, it makes sense, as two factors collide: one, the 2010 Census Bureau report that one out of every six workers is foreign born—the highest number since before the Great Depression—and, two, the staggering unemployment rate. The only way to find our bearings is to slowdown the immigration train.

An immigration moratorium does not mean we will not allow a single immigrant into this country. We would still welcome spouses of U.S. citizens, people of extraordinary ability, those with a humanitarian need, and a few other immigration categories. However, we should cut off employment-based work permits until Americans are back on their feet and slow the chain migration process for extended families.

Roy Beck, who supports a moratorium, testified at a congressional forum where he recommended that we cut the 75,000 permanent work visas issued every month to as close to zero as possible as long as the overall unemployment rate remains above 5 percent. "The numbers demand the introduction of legislation to suspend the issuance of as many permanent work visas as possible during this jobs depression," he declared.

That is my view as well. American workers need a chance to get back on their feet, and they can't accomplish this as long as a flood of new immigrants are taking jobs they've fought so hard to get.

WHY A MORATORIUM IS GOOD IN PRINCIPLE

The history of immigration reduction movements is as old as the United States, but in modern times they have gained new momentum. A distinguishing characteristic of the modern immigration reduction movement is that it not only targets illegal aliens but also seeks to rein in legal immigration policies that have led to an unhealthy population explosion. That's where the idea of a temporary moratorium comes in.

In 2003, the Congressional Immigration Reform Caucus introduced the Mass Immigration Reduction Act, which called for a five-year moratorium on most categories of immigration, with strict limitations to others. The effect of the bill would have been to reduce the annual level from 1.2 million immigrants per year to around 300,000. Further amendments to the bill suggested a cap at 100,000 immigrants per year.

The bill placed a time-out on most immigration by:

1. Halting the immigration of extended relatives of individuals who are not U.S. citizens. This includes categories such as brothers, sisters, parents, and adult children while preserving nuclear-family migration of spouses and minor children.
2. Reducing the number of employment-sponsored visas while preserving 5,000 visas for priority workers.
3. Eliminating the unwise and unnecessary diversity lottery, which awards 55,000 visas each year by a random lottery.
4. Giving immigrant status only to the children and spouses of U.S. citizens or priority workers.
5. Maintain refugee admissions and asylum adjustments to 60,000 per year. (Someone escaping the dictatorship of Robert Mugabe from Zimbabwe should be allowed into the United States, but our policy should be to remove Mugabe and try him for crimes against humanity.)

Proponents of the bill argued that only a mass moratorium could provide a wake-up call to the American public and force the open-borders lobby to justify the need and purpose of such high annual rates. Among the advantages of the moratorium:

- It would allow the Bureau of Citizenship and Immigration Services to analyze the huge backlog (more than five million) of immigrants who have applied for permanent residence status and weed out potential terrorists, criminals, and those applying fraudulently.
- It would dramatically reduce the family magnet of chain migration that not only overwhelms the nation with low-income immigrants but also encourages illegal immigration.
- It would save roughly $90 billion a year (net) in the cost of immigration.
- It would help unemployed Americans by stopping the flooding of the labor pool.
- It would temporarily halt amnesty efforts for illegal aliens.
- It would stabilize the population, thus helping the nation devise a saner environmental policy.

The bill had wide-ranging support among many groups who saw it as a necessary step toward a better immigration policy. It would also have enabled assimilation of people already here. Contrary to the popular conception that legal immigration is limited, there is no real cap on new green card issuance. This is because there are categories of immigration that are exempted or omitted from the immigration limits. The largest of these categories is visas for parents, spouses, and children of U.S. citizens, as well as adoptions. Another category is refugees and people seeking asylum, subject to a separate limit decided annually. A moratorium would likely continue those categories at some reasonable level while examining others that are deemed less essential. I advocate a population-neutral immigration approach, which I think makes a lot of sense. "Population neutral" means establishing a level of immigration that balances the number of people coming in and the number of people going out. Remember: people *do* leave the United States to live elsewhere!

Immigrant Admissions by the Numbers

The following table shows the average annual number of new green cards issued by five-year period beginning in the 1960s. The first period, 1961–1965, was prior to the adoption of the 1965 Immigration Act, which eliminated the immigration restrictions that had been in place since the early 1920s. The effects of the 1965 opening up of immigration did not begin immediately but showed some impact during the 1966–1970 period. There have been various amendments to the immigration law since 1965 that have also contributed to the upward trend, in particular legislation enacted in 1990 that increased both family-sponsored and employer-sponsored immigration and established the lottery visa system.

Annual Average Admissions

1961–1965	290,062
1966–1970	374,273
1971–1975	387,256
1976–1980	511,407
1981–1985	572,881
1986–1990	894,731
1991–1995*	784,257
1996–2000	773,021
2001–2005	982,825
2006–2008	1,141,936

Source: *FAIR*

Hampered by the open-borders preference of President George W. Bush and a nervous Congress that feared a loss of Hispanic votes in the 2004 election, the bill did not pass. However, the idea of an immigration moratorium has gained new momentum in the wake of the financial crisis. It is in that spirit that

I propose a new plan that resolves some of the conflicts surrounding previous moratorium efforts.

Eliminate the visa lottery

An easy form of immigration reduction would be to completely eliminate the senseless visa lottery, also called diversity visas. The visa lottery was established by the Immigration Act of 1990 in an attempt to bring individuals to the United States from countries that were underrepresented—as if by diversifying the pool, it would improve the quality of the melting pot. Currently, 55,000 foreign nationals per year are awarded visas to come and live permanently in the United States under the visa lottery program.

The motivation behind the visa lottery never made any sense to me. What exactly is the value of immigration diversity? Why are we encouraging people to come here from countries that the numbers would suggest are not that interested? There are worse problems. This program has so many holes you could make Swiss cheese. Even the bipartisan Barbara Jordan Commission in 1995 recommended the elimination of the lottery and said it served no national interest.

The random nature of the lottery reduces our ability to assert control over who is entering the country and presents a national security risk. The program is notorious for how easily it can be gamed. Fraud is widespread. A recent report released by the Center for Immigration Studies states that it is commonplace for foreign nationals to apply for the lottery program multiple times by using many different aliases and other false personal information.

The Department of State, Office of Visa Services, has also reported an increase in fraudulent e-mails and letters sent to visa lottery applicants. The scammers behind these fraudulent messages pose as the U.S. government in an attempt to extract payment from the applicants. In addition, the visa lottery program has spawned a cottage industry featuring sponsors in the United States who falsely promise success to applicants in exchange for large sums of money. Ill-informed foreign nationals are willing to pay top dollar for the "guarantee" of lawful permanent resident status in the United States.

In her April 2011 testimony before the House Judiciary Subcommittee on Immigration, Janice Kephart, a former counsel for the National Commission on Terrorist Attacks on the United States, told Congress, "The Diversity Visa Program is an unfortunate blind spot in our immigration system that has outlived whatever purpose it might have had. The applicants for these 50,000 [now 55,000] visa lottery immigration slots require few skills. Neither their qualifications nor identity can be properly vetted. The program does not know, really, who these applicants are or their true purpose in coming to the United States. The program is a national security vulnerability, and has been used by terrorists and organized criminals to not only enter the United States, but to bring others in as well."

Kephart pointed out that according to the State Department's own accounting, the program's standards are so low that fraud is inevitable. In most of the eligible countries, it is virtually impossible to verify work experience or education, and U.S. embassies in these areas are ill equipped to verify identity. Kephart's conclusion: the diversity lottery is a national security threat.

Let's get rid of this pointless program. It's a mess and impossible to manage.

SAMPLE Immigration Moratorium Resolution

Americans have a moral obligation first to provide opportunities to our fellow citizens, including our own working poor, homeless, and unemployed and our struggling middle class:

WHEREAS, the majority of U.S. population growth is from mass immigration (1.2 million legal immigrants and 300,000–400,000 illegals annually);

WHEREAS, the net cost of mass immigration to U.S. taxpayers is ____ (after subtracting taxes immigrants paid);

> **WHEREAS**, mass immigration costs U.S. workers jobs and depresses wages through job competition;
>
> **WHEREAS**, population growth generated by mass immigration causes increasing pressures on our environment and forces local governments and communities to spend taxpayer dollars for additional schools, healthcare facilities, waste disposal plants, transportation systems, fire protection, water supplies, power generation plants, and many other items;
>
> **WHEREAS**, a majority of Americans of all ethnic and racial backgrounds favor substantial reductions in immigration.
>
> **NOW, THEREFORE**, (print name of entity) (print city, county, state)
>
> **HEREBY RESOLVES**: that the U.S. Congress and Obama administration immediately act to end mass immigration by enacting a temporary five-year immigration moratorium on all immigration in excess of 75,000 per year, followed by an act that will allow continued immigration at sustainable levels, estimated at 300,000 per year, the number approximately equal to annual emigration.

My plan: moratorium, yes; tourists, even better

My plan is a surefire way of controlling immigration and at the same time boosting the economy with an infusion of billions of dollars. The idea is simple: start with a five-year moratorium on immigration and at the same time expand and extend the B-2 tourist visa program.

The B-2 tourist visa is a nonimmigrant visa that allows foreign nationals to enter the United States temporarily for a variety of purposes, including visiting family and friends, seeking medical treatment, business, and tourism. The B-2 visa is usually limited to one month, and to receive it, the traveler must demonstrate his or her intention to return home by showing proof of residence and binding ties.

I recommend that we expand the B-2 visa to three months and encourage multiple entries so that travelers can visit family frequently without moving here and using entitlements such as Medicare and Medicaid, which should be reserved for citizens and permanent residents.

An added benefit to this program would be a huge windfall in tourism. It is estimated that the average tourist spends $3,000 during one month in the United States. If B-2 visas were extended to three months, tourists would spend even more.

For the sake of a conservative estimate, let's say 20 million tourists extended their stays and spent $6,000 instead of $3,000—a net gain of $3,000 per tourist. That would mean $120 billion more money spent in the U.S. economy.

This is a workable plan for those who have family in the United States but who would be precluded by the moratorium from applying for residency during the five-year period. They can visit as frequently as they like, without draining jobs and services here.

Moratorium by the Numbers

CURRENT LEGAL IMMIGRANTS:	1 MILLION PER YEAR
FIVE-YEAR TOTAL:	5 MILLION
DURING THE FIVE-YEAR MORATORIUM:	100,000 PER YEAR
FIVE-YEAR MORATORIUM TOTAL:	500,000
DIRECT REDUCTION IN FIVE YEARS:	4,500,000

MONITOR ENTRY-EXIT

Of course, my plan for combining an immigration moratorium with promotion of tourist visas would work only if serious attention were paid to our entry-exit systems. We have to make sure that people are coming to the United States for their stated reasons and that they leave when their visas expire. According to a Pew Hispanic Center study, nearly half of illegal aliens arrived legally with temporary nonimmigrant visas. The Department of Homeland Security estimates that up to 57 percent of America's illegal population is made up of visa overstays—although a Government Accountability Office report suggests that this percentage underestimates the number. The point is that visa overstays represent a big problem.

In 2004, the Department of Homeland Security instituted the U.S. Visitor Immigration Status Indicator Technology (US-VISIT), a program designed to monitor entry and exits of nonimmigrant visitors and workers. The intent of US-VISIT was to use advanced biometric technology and enhanced lookout lists to improve the screening of foreign visitors, thereby helping deter and detect the entry of terrorists, criminals, immigration violators, and other dangerous or ineligible visitors. US-VISIT performs three functions:

- It authenticates the identity of visitors, that is, makes sure that the visitor is the same person who was issued the documents presented, thus guarding against document and identity fraud.
- It screens visitors against a new array of expanded security and immigration watch lists.
- It records entries and exits of visitors and enables authorities to know whether a visitor has departed and complied with the terms of admission.

US-VISIT has been slow to get off the ground fully, and, to date, there is no effective program that verifies when someone leaves the country. Officials estimate that 2.9 million foreigners overstayed their visas last year. These statistics drive home the point that huge numbers of foreign nationals are succeeding in convincing American consular officers that they are bona fide tourists when, in fact, they are immigrants.

Programs such as US-VISIT are essential management tools for the moratorium program, but they have to work better to track visitors as they come and go. Privatizing the task of monitoring the millions of visitors to the United States should also be an option. This new company would be floated on either the

NYSE or NASDAQ, and we the public would be shareholders. As long as the company did its job, the public would continue to hold shares of the company in its portfolios. Performance would be tied to results.

The American economy would receive an enormous boost if we cut back on immigrant visas and instead focused on the issuance of visitors' visas—another form of family reunification without the cost to American taxpayers. It's a win-win for everyone. As Roy Beck said, "A time-out on most immigration would not solve the nation's budget crisis. But it would stop immigration from making matters worse. Plus, a time-out on most immigration would mean that hundreds of thousands of unemployed Americans who would not otherwise get back to work would do so in the first year alone. That would be a huge victory for those Americans and a modest reduction in expenditures by taxpayers to support them."

The United States must continue to leave the door open for people to enter this great land and see for themselves what makes America unique. This can be done without burdening our already weakened economy through a combination of a five year moratorium alongside a generous B-2 visitor visa program.

Chapter 11

Step Four—End Family Reunification

Chain migration . . . is one of the fundamental reasons why our businesses have problems sponsoring legal immigrants, why our federal caseworkers have problems with paperwork backlogs, and why our system has become so frustrating that individuals outside the United States would rather risk immigrating here illegally than wait forever in line.

—Representative Phil Gingrey

The impact of our nation's family reunification policy often gets lost in the discussions of immigration reform, yet it is the umbilical cord, the primary pathway through which millions of people are added to the rolls every decade, regardless of their ability to contribute to the growth and prosperity of the nation. Before the family reunification legislation was enacted in 1965, there were quotas, and the family members affected were limited to first-tier relatives.

Today, the seemingly endless chain is strangling our immigration system as extended family members clog waiting lists to enter. It doesn't make sense to me that an immigrant who willingly comes to this country should automatically be allowed to bring his or her extended family as well.

Chain migration is often referred to as a "family values" policy. Ira Mehlman, a spokesman for FAIR, disagrees. "What we ought to have is an immigration policy that recognizes the sanctity of the nuclear family—spouses and unmarried minor children—but we simply cannot promise immigration entitlements to every member of your extended family," he said. "It's unachievable because everybody is related to somebody."

Barbara Jordan's Commission on Immigration Reform studied the issue of chain migration in the 1990s and proposed limiting family-sponsored immigration to only the spouse and minor children of a U.S. citizen or a legal permanent resident and the parents of a U.S. citizen, as long as they are supported by the sponsor, with a ceiling of 400,000 per year. What would be cut would be visas for siblings of U.S. citizens and adult sons and daughters of both U.S. citizens and legal permanent residents. "A properly regulated system of legal immigration is in the national interest of the United States," the commission wrote. "Such a system enhances the benefits of immigration while protecting against potential harms. Unless there is a compelling national interest to do otherwise, immigrants should be chosen on the basis of the skills they contribute to the U.S. economy. The Commission believes that admission of nuclear family members and refugees provide such a compelling national interest. Reunification of adult children and siblings of adult citizens solely because of their family relationship is not as compelling." Needless to say, the commission's recommendation was never adopted.

In 2007 and again in 2009, Representative Phil Gingrey introduced the Nuclear Family Priority Act, which would have eliminated certain extended-family categories. When he first introduced the legislation, Gingrey testified before the House Judiciary Committee and explained the cost of the current chain migration system. "The 1965 immigration preference system, and subsequent modifications, including the 1990 Immigration Act, expanded immigration levels far beyond traditional levels, mostly by prioritizing extended family members," he said. "Our immigration system is obviously out of kilter when one immigrant can yield upwards of 273 other legal immigrants in as short as 15 years, assuming the average birthrate of the developing world. It is hard to believe one immigrant of skill or humanitarian need could yield so many dependants under our laws of family reunification, yet the only limits on our current chain system are age and death. Assuming everyone in an immigrant's family wants to immigrate to the United States and they are all alive, this 273 number is a real possibility."

Think about it: 11 million illegal immigrants × 273 = 3 billion people in 15 years! This is what amnesty will produce.

Even if Gingrey's estimate of 273 people in a single immigrant's chain is extreme, just two-thirds or half that number would be equally scary. This is a policy that we cannot afford to continue. Furthermore, if amnesty programs such as the DREAM Act were to become law, the effect would be dramatic. It is estimated that the DREAM Act would provide amnesty to anywhere between 1.1 and 2 million illegal aliens. But, according to Professor Stanley Renshon, an immigration authority, "The end result of that DREAM Act, if it had been passed, would be probably 6 to 7 million aliens because we have chain migration in this country. Once you become a naturalized citizen, you can sponsor your parents, your brothers and sisters, your spouses, your children and once all of them are in, they can do the same for their families and once their families are in, their families can do the same for their families." So, I say yes to the DREAM Act and no to family reunification.

As Jon Feere pointed out in a recent report by the Center for Immigration Studies, "Family-sponsored immigration accounts for most of the nation's growth in immigration levels. Of the 1,130,818 immigrants who were granted legal permanent residency in 2009, a total of 747,413 (or, 66.1 percent) were family-sponsored immigrants. . . . This number continues to rise every year because of the ever-expanding migration chains that operate independently of any economic downturns or labor needs. Although automatic and universal birthright citizenship is not the only contributor to chain migration, ending it would prevent some of this explosive growth."

RESET THE CHAIN

I propose that we begin a process to return migration to its pre-1965 status and limit the chain to immediate family members, that is, spouses and underage children. We can begin doing this by eliminating three categories:

1. Adult brothers and sisters: estimated number, 65,000 per year
2. Married sons and daughters: estimated number, 23,400 per year
3. Unmarried adult sons and daughters: estimated number, 23,400 per year

   Total reduction: 111,800 per year

With this plan, we would reduce the number by 1,118,000 over 10 years and completely eliminate the massive backlog that currently exists. Congress has the ability—if it has the nerve—to do this.

Eliminate the anchor

We have already seen how so-called birthright citizenship has opened the door to some 350,000 new citizens a year—infants born to illegal aliens. These new American babies then become the anchor for the family chains. So you don't have just 350,000 new residents: even if the chain for each of these infants was limited to two parents, two siblings, four grandparents, and four aunts and uncles (12)—which we know is a ridiculously low number—the number would be not 350,000 but more than four million!

The Baby Chain

350,000 infants
+ 2 parents = 1,050,000
+ 2 siblings = 1,750,000
+ 4 grandparents = 3,150,000
+ 4 aunts and uncles = 4,550,000
TOTAL: 4,550,000

Perhaps the biggest obstacle to eliminating birthright citizenship for the offspring of illegals is the belief that such a move would require a constitutional amendment—an almost impossible bar to reach. However, a growing number of legal scholars disagree, concluding that nothing in the plain language of the Fourteenth Amendment would require the present expansive interpretation of birthright citizenship and noting that the peculiar phrase in Section 1 referring to persons who are "subject to the jurisdiction thereof" would, in fact, seem to imply otherwise. Taking their cue from this, for more than 15 years, various senators and members of Congress have periodically and unsuccessfully attempted to pass legislation clarifying the reach of the amendment to exclude children unless they are born of U.S. citizens or resident aliens. The legislation has gone nowhere.

Frustrated by the lack of progress on the federal level and believing that we should not grant birthright citizenship to the offspring of people who have no legitimate status in America, the states have taken up the cause. In January 2011, legislators from five states introduced legislation aimed at eliminating automatic citizenship for the offspring of illegals. Officials from Pennsylvania, Arizona, Oklahoma, Georgia, South Carolina, and other states said they were taking aim at birthright citizenship by seeking to apply the Constitution's Fourteenth Amendment only to children with at least one parent who is a permanent resident or citizen. They acknowledged that they didn't see much hope of the legislation passing but were hopeful of starting a process that would force the issue to be examined by the Supreme Court.

There is little question that birthright citizenship is indeed headed to the highest court, where it may gain a receptive audience. The time is right for commonsense policies that don't chain us to the past. I would encourage Congress to pull its head out of the sand and weigh in on this critical issue.

Encourage one-off migration

A fascinating article by David North for the Center for Immigration Studies got me thinking about another simple and obvious way to address the destructive cycle of chain migration. North suggested that we institute a policy to give preference to "one-offs"—that is, otherwise eligible immigrants who would pledge not to have children or petition for other family members. North referred to some obvious categories of people that would be candidates for the one-off: Catholic priests and nuns, older people (with assured pensions and healthcare programs), and partners of gay and lesbian legal residents. (The latter would be free to adopt within the United States, as that would not add to the count.)

In presenting his idea, North wrote, "If you are worried about too many people in our inner cities, too much farmland gobbled up by suburban sprawl, too many pressures on our decaying infrastructure, then you might think of these one-offs as the most desirable of all immigrants. My suggestion is that anyone otherwise eligible wanting to come to the U.S. who promised not to have children and who vowed not to seek admission of any other immigrants should be placed at the head of the waiting line, and that their admissions would substitute for people in the family preference categories (other than immediate relatives of citizens who are not numerically controlled anyway)."

I don't think North was being the least bit facetious about this idea. In its own way, it's a brilliant reversal on family reunification policies, which have paralyzed us for decades.

Ask what immigrants can do for us

A fascinating new book offers a compelling case for changing the immigration emphasis from family reunification to value-added, prosperity-enhancing standards. *Beside the Golden Door: Immigration Reform in a New Era of Globalization*, by Pia Orrenius and Madeline Zavodny, presents a refreshing idea—that immigrants should be givers as well as takers and that our immigration policies should dare to ask, "What can you do for us?"

The authors state that it makes no sense for the United States to continue to lavish green cards on far-flung extended families at the expense of highly skilled or wealthy foreigners who can contribute to our economic growth. They point out that in no other advanced economy is such low priority given to high-end workers who can make healthy contributions to the tax base and the overall economy. About 85 percent of green cards are issued to family members, for humanitarian purposes, and in the visa lottery. That leaves 15 percent for workers, of which half are family members. So only 7 percent of green cards are issued with economic benefits in mind. Orrenius and Zavodny recommend, among other measures, the institution of lotteries where companies can bid for permits to bring in foreign workers, mostly in highly skilled capacities. The system and the number of permits would be sensitive to the economy, a significant change over the current system that is completely nonresponsive to economic ups and downs.

I'll go a step further and suggest that we should create an investment category that gives preferential status to those who are capable of bringing investment, creating businesses, and hiring American workers. It's time to put an end to a system that burdens America's fragile economy in favor of one that boosts its chances for growth.

Actually, it's a little-known fact (because it's not well advertised) that the United States has special immigration laws on the books for investors from the outside. The E-2 visa is a nonimmigrant visa for investors purchasing an existing business or establishing a new business in the United States. Investments are normally required to be a minimum of $100,000–$150,000—but can be much more—and the investor must demonstrate that the business will generate more than enough income to support the investor and the investor's family and will also contribute to the economy, usually by employing U.S. workers.

We should actively seek out wealthy investors who have made their fortunes transparently (as opposed to criminal activity or corruption) and make them citizens or give them green cards because it creates jobs and brings capital to our country. It would be a net gain. Imagine if instead of the 30 million–plus immigrants we have allowed into our country we had given just one million E-2 investor visas at $1 million apiece. That would be a $1-trillion capital injection in addition to a boost for local economies.

According to Boston Consulting Group, global wealth outside the United States stands at $97 trillion. While some of this money is already in the United States in the form of investments (stock, bonds, etc.), an aggressive push to expand and extend the E-2 visa to cover just 5 percent of this total is $4.85 trillion into the country. Alternatively, if we issue one million visas to attract millionaires (to park $1 million) and give them a path to citizenship, we are looking at $1,000,000,000,000 (yes, one trillion dollars).

In a 2011 report titled "Global Talent Risks: Seven Responses," the Boston Consulting Group warned that a severe talent crisis awaits industrialized, high-tech nations by 2020, with a growing need for highly educated, technologically sophisticated workers. Is that our future as a nation? I have to wonder what vision we have for ourselves when the majority of immigrants we allow here each year are poorly educated, low-skill workers.

America's out-of-control immigration policy should be addressed immediately by both the Congress and the White House, before our country becomes the Balkanized States of America instead of the United States of America.

Chapter 12

Step Five— Love Thy Neighbor

Foreign aid is neither a failure nor a panacea. It is, instead, an important tool of American policy that can serve the interests of the United States and the world if wisely administered.

—Lee H. Hamilton

Not long ago, for the sake of discussion, I asked a random group of U.S. citizens whether, given the choice, they would want to live in a different country. I didn't specify which country, just offered them their choice of any other place in the world. I didn't really expect an overwhelming interest in leaving, but I thought maybe a handful of people would want to go. That was not the case. I didn't get a single taker in my experiment. Why? Because, with all our failings, America is still a great place to live and most citizens agree that it is the best country in the world.

Contrast that with Mexico. According to the Pew Foundation, 33 percent of immigration-age citizens in Mexico—about 23 million people—have said they would like to live in the United States, and of these, nearly 13 million have said they would do it even if they weren't legalized. That's just one country, and the desire is duplicated in many countries of Central and South America.

This, in a nutshell, is the problem: humanity, on the whole, longs for freedom, the rule of law, a stable community in which to raise families, basic services, and a belief in the future. America represents that potential, while too many countries are consumed by poverty, violence, corruption, and despair. You can't really blame people for wanting to use any means necessary to flee their situations and better their lives. But as Roy Beck illustrated so vividly in his gumball experiment, we cannot save the suffering peoples of the world by bringing them here. The only viable way to express our compassion and our commitment to global progress is to find ways of helping them do better *there*.

This idea is not unprecedented. In 1947, in a grand gesture of goodwill and economic development, the United States created the Marshall Plan, named after Secretary of State George Marshall. The four-year plan involved pouring $13 billion into the redevelopment of European nations that had been devastated in World War II. In a now-celebrated speech delivered at Harvard

University on June 5, 1947, Marshall heralded the plan as a solution to the widespread hunger, unemployment, and housing shortages that faced Europeans in the aftermath of World War II. Marshall's address was the culmination of increasing U.S. concern over the disintegrating European situation. Marshall, with the full support of President Truman, made the case that a broken Europe would be a peril to the entire planet. In other words, we Americans helped ourselves by helping them.

Reflecting on our current predicament, I realized that the situation we face south of our border is just as devastating as that in post-War Europe. Mexico, as we have discussed in previous chapters, is a failed state whose residents flood our nation because they cannot survive at home.

SAVING MEXICO

What can be done to shore up Mexico's fortunes and make it a good neighbor for the United States? What are the means by which a city such as Tijuana can equal its neighbor San Diego in wealth and civic vitality?

Mexico is one of the world's largest producers of petroleum. It has abundant resources of natural gas and other valuable minerals. It has very hardworking people. It has an indigenous culture. It has a lush landscape conducive for tourism. It is a unique nation. There is no reason that Mexico should be poor other than corrupt governance and the influence of enormous drug cartels.

There are those who live very well in Mexico, but the majority of the population is poor. The Mexican government has avoided revolution in Mexico by simply opening up its borders. All of those who might otherwise be potential opponents of the government and engage in putting constant pressure on the government aren't in Mexico. Instead, they're here—in the streets of the United States. They live in every state of the union now instead of demanding justice from their officials. Concomitantly, organizations such as the Salvation Army and church groups across the nation work tirelessly to provide the soup kitchens and food pantries that are emptied by feeding and clothing those escaping the injustice of the Mexican system.

But this show of benevolence may be exactly the opposite of what we need to do to help Mexico solve its problems. In a strongly worded appeal in *The Washington Post*, Edward Schumacher-Matos called for U.S. military intervention in a situation that has become impossible to control by standard law enforcement measures. "Seven criminal cartels effectively control most cities and the drug trafficking lanes near its borders, as well as the bases and production centers in the interior," he wrote. Although President Felipe Calderon has tried (valiantly, Schumacher-Matos suggests) to wage war on the cartels, thousands of retribution murders attest to the failure of his efforts.

Schumacher-Matos is among the voices calling for a dose of American military might. "Call in the Marines!" he urges in what would once have been an unthinkable plea. He points to a similar effort in Columbia that has had some success, involving U.S. military trainers and intelligence officers working side-by-side with nationals.

The point is that violence cannot stand as the signature of a nation, especially when that nation is on our border and is sending a steady stream of its citizens into our communities. Those who express horror at the idea of military intervention should think again.

Let me be clear. My goal is not to single out Mexicans in the United States or Hispanics in general. The fact is that if we replaced Mexico with Iran or Pakistan or Russia, we would be telling the same story. The citizens of Iran would escape the dictatorship of the clerics to find a new lease on life in America, and Pakistanis and Russians would escape the corruption of their systems to give their children a hope for a better future. The distinction is that Mexico is our neighbor. We have a semi-failed state on our southern border that needs our help.

CONDUCT A DRUG LEGALIZATION EXPERIMENT

I have never consumed alcohol or used drugs of any type, and I do not smoke. Therefore, in principal, I am against legalization of substances, such as drugs, that can affect our mind and behavior. And yet, there is a case to be made that a drug legalization experiment could actually stabilize our border communities and Mexico.

A major reason Mexico is a failed state is the power of drug cartels, which create fear and terror along the border and insinuate themselves into the law enforcement and political culture in Mexico. In spite of U.S. aid in the billions of dollars to fight the drug war, no progress has been made for an obvious reason: as long as the product is illegal, it will be supported by a violent underground economy. Rendering the cartels powerless by taking away the profits they gain from the sale of drugs should be the focus.

During the 2010 debate over Proposition 19, a California measure to legalize marijuana, opponents scoffed at the idea that it would make any difference to Mexican cartels. Yet according to reports published in *The Washington Post* and elsewhere, the cartels are said to be deeply worried about how legalization in the states would affect their profits. In a 2010 report by the Latin American Commission on Drugs and Democracy, former presidents of Mexico, Colombia, and Brazil called for discussion on legalizing marijuana and noted, "Prohibitionist policies based on the eradication of production and on the disruption of drug flows as well as on the criminalization of consumption have not yielded the expected results. We are farther than ever from the announced goal of eradicating drugs." They add that corruption and violence have increased throughout the region as a result of the strategy.

John Walker of justsaynow.com wrote, "If drugs, like marijuana, were legal, there would be no black market, no black market profits with which to buy military-style weapons, and no need to use military weapons to protect the black market businesses." Walker said that up to 60 percent of all cartel revenue comes from marijuana.

An exhaustive 2010 Rand Corporation study, while acknowledging the difficulty of accurately calculating the costs associated with marijuana trafficking from Mexico, stated quite clearly that marijuana legalization in California alone would dramatically cut drug cartel profits. The report summarized the impact this way:

We believe that legalizing marijuana in California would effectively eliminate Mexican DTOs' [cartels'] revenues from supplying Mexican-grown marijuana to the California market. As we elaborate in this chapter, even with taxes, legally produced marijuana would likely cost no more than would illegal marijuana from Mexico and would cost less than half as much per unit of THC (Kilmer, Caulkins, Pacula, et al., 2010). Thus, the needs of the California market would be supplied by the new legal industry. While, in theory, some DTO employees might choose to work in the legal marijuana industry, they would not be able to generate unusual profits, nor be able to draw on talents that are particular to a criminal organization.

We also believe that Mexican DTOs would eventually lose all revenue stemming from the selling of Mexican marijuana to underage users in California. When it becomes possible in California for anyone over the age of 21 to provide juveniles with marijuana that is cheaper, better, and subject to more quality control, Mexican DTOs will have no more competitive advantage than they would trying to sell alcohol and cigarettes to California youth today.

Despite my personal reservations—on moral and ethical grounds—I believe it's time to take a serious look at steps that render drug cartels powerless, in the hope that it will then result in eliminating the plague of violence on our border.

MICROFINANCE: THE GOLDEN DOOR

In my discussions with illegal workers in the parking lot of Home Depot, one thing is consistent: they *really* want to go home. During our conversations, I threw out various ideas for what would make them content to settle in their own countries. It always boiled down to jobs and economics.

An idea has been percolating with me for some time that may seem wild to some people but makes complete economic sense. Consider that we already pour billions of dollars into aid for Mexico and Latin America, on top of additional billions used to fight the drug war, and yet our money seems to fall into a bottomless pit of corruption and misuse. Perhaps it's time to enlist the wealthy investors of the world to create a microfinance banking system that would boost the fortunes of small businesses in the region.

There is a precedent for this. Dr. Muhammad Yunus, founder of Grameen Bank, pioneered the idea in his homeland of Bangladesh after witnessing the devastating famines of the 1970s. An economist in America, Yunus believed that there could be a business solution to failing nations. Yunus saw that his people were hardworking and motivated but their economic plight made it impossible to get started. He created a new path to wealth called microloans. He started Grameen Bank to provide small interest-free loans to villagers in Bangladesh. Today, his bank lends half a billion dollars a year, and in 2006, Yunus won a Nobel Peace Price. That's leadership that makes a difference!

I can imagine a similar setup in Mexico and certain Latin American countries that would inspire residents to stay and prosper instead of fleeing. When I pose such a plan to illegal aliens hanging out in my community and trying to find work, their eyes light up. Yes, they say, they would return home if they could get a loan for $2,000, $5,000, or $10,000 to start their own community businesses. These microfinance setups could be privately established, using Yunus's bank as a model. A one-time capital raise of $200 billion ($10,000 x 20 million aliens in the U.S.) would allow for micro-loans to 20 million Mexicans, Central Americans, Indians, Pakistanis and Africans currently in the U.S. to go back to their homelands and start new lives.

In addition, the U.S. can establish a mini-China south of the border that would encourage manufacturing and growth. Currently, the United States imports $364.9 billion in goods from China. My question is, How can we create an environment in our own region that would flourish and produce goods at the same level? De-coupling American consumers from Chinese products and refocusing purchases from Mexico, Central and Latin America would create sustainable jobs to the south and still allow for relatively cheap products to be purchased by American consumers. Indeed, wage differentials between China and Mexico/Central America are not that great. A shorter distance to market in the U.S. should encourage American companies such as Apple to move their assembly operations away from China and into Mexico/Central America.

Once again, the example of Costa Rica is instructive. In 1996 Intel chose this tiny country to locate its $300 million semiconductor plant and assembly facility. The impact of Intel's move on Costa Rica's gross domestic product, foreign direct investment and trade growth has been such that today the country has become a magnet for more investment and hence, job creation. Foreign direct investment was $336 million in 1996; by 2004 it was $585 million and today it is $1.4 billion. As Costa Ricans are proud to say, "We export goods not humans."

Investment is crucial to revitalizing our southern neighbors, and there are signs of hope—including in Mexico, as the chart below shows.

New Investment in Mexico: Signs of Hope

International investment in Mexico is critical to its growth and economic vitality. Here are a few major projects that were under way in 2011.

COMPANY	INVESTMENT	PROJECT
General Motors	$540 million	Plant expansion in Toluca
General Motors	$300 million	Plant upgrades in San Luis Potosi
Tenaris (Dubai)	$30 million	New plant to manufacture pumping rods for steel pipe manufacturing
Hutchison Port Holdings	$200 million	Improvements at Port of Lazaro Cardenas
Furniture Brands	$20 million	Outfitting existing plant to manufacture cut-and-sew kits
Nissan	$900 million	Increased auto production at plants in Aguascalientes and Morelos
Magna International	$100 million	New auto parts plant in San Luis Potosi

Source: *Mexico Business Blog, February 9, 2011*

More promising still, beginning in 2009, the Latin America and Mid-East Investment Forum in Abu Dhabi has become center stage for a futuristic approach to creating wealth in Latin America. The conference, which is in its third year as I write this, brings together delegations from Latin American corporations and financial institutions with potential investors from GCC (Gulf Cooperation Council) states—Bahrain, Kuwait, Oman, Qatar, Saudi Arabia, and the United Arab Emirates.

With their rich natural resources, Latin American states, such as Argentina, Brazil, Chile, Colombia, Mexico, and Peru, provide a fertile ground for investment—especially for the GCC countries that are eager to plant a stake in promising parts of the world.

I believe that investment is the key to the future stability and prosperity of our southern neighbors, and the wealthy GCC nations are the perfect sponsors. In the past decade, Persian Gulf states have invested more than $25 billion in Latin America, including exports and investments in raw minerals and agriculture. I can conceive of a partnership between the wealthy countries of the Persian Gulf (with more than $1 trillion in wealth), the U.S. government, and the Latin American private sector—with the Gulf nations investing in manufacturing plants in Latin America, which would then sell their merchandise in the United States, thus creating a win-win for everyone. Here is a concrete example. Last year the U.S. imported $8 billion worth of toys from China. Asking the GCC to invest in plants that manufacture toys in Mexico or El Salvador would mean sustainable jobs south of the border and an established market (American consumers) for export. The GCC investors would be guaranteed a long-term source of revenue from selling toys into the U.S. market, jobs would be created and sustained south of the border, and America would benefit in two ways: less immigration and cheap toys. Mixing economics with immigration policy is common sense.

Export educated illegals

Recently, Maryland's governor, Martin O'Malley, proposed allowing the state's illegal immigrants to pay in-state tuition to attend the state's public universities, at the anticipated cost of $3.5 million over five years. Similar legislation has been floated in other states and places an additional burden on already struggling economies. It is questionable whether O'Malley's idea will survive the controversy and rash of lawsuits. However, I would propose a compromise: if advocates insist that taxpayers should subsidize the education of illegal immigrants, then we must also insist that once they complete their studies, they return to their home countries to serve and rebuild. Then we could consider it money well spent to invest in the prosperity of our neighbors.

In the 1960s, the government of Iran established the Education Corps and Health Corps, made up of young men and women with college degrees who served their country by teaching reading and writing and by administering health care. This model can be duplicated in America, especially on the southern border, with illegal immigrant children who take advantage of in-state tuition leniency to get degrees at American colleges. I believe that eligibility should be contingent on their willingness to then return to their homelands and help in economic development. This way, an educated Salvadoran or Mexican or Ghanaian can contribute to the socio-economic situation of his or her country by taking advantage of the generosity of American taxpayers. This program might be supervised by the Peace Corps or U.S. AID.

Sensible compassion

The United States is a wealthy nation, and there is much we can do for the struggling people south of our border—means of support that do not include bringing them into our country. Roger Winters, director of the U.S. Committee for Refugees, has said that the cost of settling one refugee in the United States could cover the expenses of 500 refugees abroad. To me, that says it all.

Though we may be the greatest oak in the greatest forest, we can produce enough acorns to feed only so many. Do we deny our own to feed the world? Can we deny our own to feed the world? What is necessary is to provide great oaks that will grow and thrive in every nation of our region and beyond, that will spread the great branches of democratic principles that provide for the many, not just for the privileged few. We can enable others to experience the principles of true justice and the rule of law, protection from the privileged, the rich and powerful, the criminal and contemptible of this world. We can inspire a new beginning for the people of disadvantaged nations to our south.

Global prosperity requires a new narrative on immigration and cross-border migration. If we allow the poor to escape to the rich and then redistribute our wealth to take care of the needy new arrivals, we will only impoverish ourselves in the process. Global prosperity must increase if we are to address this issue seriously. Perhaps then our nation will not be overwhelmed by those seeking that which exists in such abundance here.

Conclusion

A More Perfect Union in 2022

The mighty tide of immigration to our shores has brought in its train much of good and much of evil; and whether the good or the evil shall predominate depends mainly on whether these newcomers do or do not throw themselves heartily into our national life.

—Theodore Roosevelt

I magine that all of my recommendations were put into practice in 2012. What would we see 10 years later in 2022? Granted, 10 years is not very long in the scheme of things, especially considering that our immigration policy has been in a constant state of crisis at least since the 1970s. Even so, if you think of immigration as a steadily leaking faucet, turning it off for 10 years, or even reducing the flow, will mean that the flooding will be stopped. This will be done not with a wrench and a hammer but with the "soft power" of persuasion and opportunity at home.

I ask you to let your thoughts stretch forward a decade and consider how dramatically things will have changed as a result of enacting my simple proposals.

Let's review the benefits of my immigration plan. Note that all of these measures are within our capabilities. This is not a pie-in-the-sky wish list but a practical vision.

- **MAKE ENGLISH THE OFFICIAL LANGUAGE**, saving the federal government and the states billions of dollars a year in multilingual systems.
- **CREATE ESL IMMERSION PROGRAMS** to more quickly get immigrants up to speed. Studies show that immersion is the most effective way to learn a language.
- **ENCOURAGE BLACK EMPOYMENT** by reducing illegal and legal immigration. The benefits to the black community could be $840 billion in one year and $8.4 trillion in ten years (if we assume full employment for blacks at $30,000 per annum for 28 million working blacks).

- **SUPPORT ON-THE-JOB ESL TRAINING** to improve the capacity of newcomers to assimilate.
- **ENFORCE THE LAWS ON THE BOOKS**, especially regarding securing the borders, cracking down on employers that hire illegal aliens, and deporting people who have overstayed their visas or who are otherwise in the country illegally.
- **MAKE E-VERIFY MANDATORY** for all businesses and agencies.
- **REQUIRE REAL ID** compliance in the states immediately, and override those (few) states that have chosen not to comply.
- **PRIVATIZE** aspects of the security technology and investigative arms of law enforcement to streamline the operations and save taxpayer dollars.
- **IMPOSE A FIVE-YEAR MORATORIUM** on legal immigration, except for high-priority categories totaling 75,000 a year.
- **REDUCE IMMIGRATION QUOTAS** at the end of the moratorium to 300,000 per year.
- **EXTEND VISITORS' VISAS** during the immigration moratorium to create a tourist boom. The tourism boost over five years: $600 billion.
- **ELIMINATE THE VISA LOTTERY**, which is a meaningless category that has national security implications, thus reducing legal immigrants by 550,000 over 10 years.
- **RESTORE PRE-1965 FAMILY REUNIFICATION POLICIES**, giving preference to nuclear families only.
- **ELIMINATE AUTOMATIC BIRTHRIGHT CITIZENSHIP**, and require that babies born in the United States have at least one parent who is a citizen or a legal resident.
- **ENCOURAGE ONE-OFF IMMIGRATION**, favoring single individuals with no family chains.
- **SUPPORT STABILIZATION AND ECONOMIC GROWTH** in the region—a Marshall Plan for Mexico/Central America.

- **EMPLOY "SOFT POWER"** through the voice of America and other means, to speak of the opportunity that exists and must be grabbed at home.
- **LEGALIZE MARIJUANA** on an experimental basis to begin the process of putting Mexican drug cartels out of business.
- **CREATE MICROFINANCE OPPORTUNITIES** in Mexico and Latin America.
- **ENCOURAGE INVESTOR VISAS**, which will create up to a trillion-dollar investment boom. This could yield $3 trillion in three years.

A DRAMATIC NUMBERS REDUCTION

From a numbers perspective, my straightforward recommendations would have an immediate result in reducing the flow of immigrants, both legal and illegal, in the following ways:

The five-year moratorium would reduce the number of immigrants from one million a year to 75,000 for five years, followed by a permanent reduction to 30,000 per year. The total reduction over a decade would be 8,125,000:

Current:

   1 million per year × 10 years = 10 million

Under moratorium and quotas:

   75,000 per year for five years = 375,000

   300,000 per year for five years = 1,500,000

Total reduction over 10 years: 8,125,000

The cancellation of the visa lottery would reduce immigration by 55,000 per year, for a 10-year reduction of **550,000**.

By eliminating extended family members from family reunification, we would realize a reduction over 10 years of **1,118,000**, based solely on the following categories:

Adult brothers and sisters = 65,000 per year

Married sons and daughters = 23,400 per year

Unmarried adult sons and daughters = 23,400 per year

Total reduction over 10 years: 1,118,000

A change in the birthright citizenship law would reduce the number of new citizens that were children of illegal aliens by about 350,000 per year, or **3,500,000** over 10 years. That number does not take into account the family members that would have been able to seek legal status through family reunification.

It is impossible to accurately gauge the number of illegal aliens that would be deported or who would self-deport if stricter enforcement were imposed— not to mention the numbers that wouldn't come here in the first place. However, even a conservative estimate in which we reduce illegal aliens by 20 percent over a decade would equal **2,400,000.**

Total reduction of immigrants, legal and illegal, by 2022: **15,693,000.**

If half of those were job holders or potential job holders, that would mean nearly eight million jobs freed up for Americans currently out of work.

A road to economic recovery

Immigration reform according to my plan would be a virtual economic windfall over 10 years. Let's start with the savings generated by reducing illegal immigrants by 20 percent and changing the law to eliminate automatic birthright citizenship:

<u>Annual cost of illegal immigrants:</u>

General costs: $113 billion per year

Anchor babies: $1.7 billion per year

Lost wages for Americans: $375 billion per year

<u>Savings over 10 years with a 20 percent reduction of illegal aliens:</u>

General costs: $2.260 billion per year × 10 years = $226 billion

Anchor babies: $1.7 billion per year × 10 years = $170 billion

Lost wages: $75 billion per year × 10 years = $750 billion

<u>Total 10-year savings with 20 percent fewer illegal aliens:</u>

$396 billion in direct costs

$750 billion in wages recovered by Americans

We would also realize significant savings if English were to become the official language. On the basis of state estimates and using Canada's bilingual system as a model, the cost of performing official functions in multiple languages is about $24 per citizen per year. That's **$7.416 billion—$741.6 billion over a decade**.

At the same time we are reducing illegal immigrants and placing a temporary moratorium on legal immigration, my plan calls for increasing the number of tourist visas, which would create a tourist boom worth approximately **$120 billion**.

Fix Immigration Create Wealth

The more people coming into the country, legally or illegally, the more we need to spend on the federal, state and local level—as this graph demonstrates.

Spending in real dollars (billions)

	Federal	State	Local	Welfare	Education
1980	$590	$173	$259	$59	$97
1990	$1.2 T	$397	$575	$96	$212
2000	$1.7 T	$757	$985	$173	$390
2010	$3.4 T	$1.3 T	$1.5 T	$502	$604

While the increases at the federal level can be attributed in part to two wars (2000-2010) and at the local level to pension benefits, it is possible that spending levels have increased for welfare and education due to an influx of new people to our population, mostly through immigration.

A PROMISE OF NATIONAL UNITY AND STRENGTH

As an economist, I often look at immigration reform as a numbers game, and, indeed, it is. As you can see by the calculations above, basic changes in immigration policy and practice would reap huge rewards. But there are other less tangible benefits that are equally crucial. These are measured by the prospect of America as a strong and peaceful nation, surrounded by neighbors that are emerging centers of economic stability, where the rule of law maintains order and the well-being of the citizenry. Our commitment to helping our southern neighbors is an important part of guaranteeing our own future. It is possible to imagine this region becoming a model to the world of what it means to prosper in a new era of financial solvency and mutual respect. That is my vision, and I believe it is well within our reach.

The essential truth is not about numbers but about human beings. We must adopt an immigration policy that serves our national interest. America's global power begins at home with a strong economy that is able to generate wealth. In short, we can solve our immigration policy and return our country to a superpower status or do nothing and become a welfare state. In the end, we have to ask ourselves, Do we want to be a nation of makers or a nation of takers?

I believe that America was built on the notion of meritocratic fairness not mediocrity. Not acting on immigration reform will turn this great nation into a mediocre country. Fixing immigration will save America and restore the promise of a better future for our children and the world.

A Case Study

Illegal Immigration Dislocates Significant Economic Activity in America

This Case Study was conducted by Sage Policy Group, Inc. of Baltimore, Maryland.

Introduction

The impact of illegal immigration to America has been widespread and profound. It is difficult to identify another aspect of American life in which the U.S. legal framework is so frequently ignored, with the possible exception of driving above the speed limit. Among other things, Section 237 of the Immigration and Nationality Act states that an alien is deportable if the alien was "inadmissible at the time of entry" (Act 237, General Classes of Deportable Aliens).

The Department of Homeland Security (DHS) estimates that between 1980 and 2009, 10.8 million unauthorized immigrants came into the United States. Exhibit 1 provides statistical detail regarding this unauthorized immigration. More than half of those who arrived in America over the past three decades came during a 10-year period stretching from 1995–2004.[1] The pace of illegal migration has slowed more recently, perhaps due to the economic downturn, which has disproportionately impacted the construction segment, a principal employer of illegal labor.

It is also worth noting that many of these illegal immigrants are young. This is not surprising since much of this population comes to America to secure employment. It is also primarily a male population, with males accounting for 62 percent of the unauthorized population in the 18 to 34 age group in 2010 according to DHS.[2]

---

1. Department of Homeland Security (2010), Estimates of the Unauthorized Immigrant Population Residing in the U.S., available at http://www.dhs.gov/xlibrary/assets/statistics/publications/ois_ill_pe_2010.pdf.
2. *Ibid.*

Exhibit 1. Unauthorized Immigrants
by Period of Entry and Select Characteristics

Period of Entry	# of Immigrants	Age	# of Immigrants
2005–2009	990,000	< 18 years	1,230,000
2000–2004	3,190,000	18–24 years	1,290,000
1995–1999	2,920,000	25–34 years	3,780,000
1990–1994	1,670,000	35–44 years	2,990,000
1985–1989	1,170,000	45–54 years	1,100,000
1980–1984	850,000	55 years and over	390,000
All years	**10,790,000**	**All ages**	**10,790,000**

Source: *Department of Homeland Security*

In 2009, the Pew Hispanic Center estimated the unauthorized immigrant population to be 11.1 million, or 3.7 percent of the nation's total population of 307 million. California had the largest number of unauthorized immigrants (2.55 million immigrants, or 6.9 percent of state population), followed by Texas at 1.6 million (6.5 percent of state population) and Florida with an estimated 675,000 illegal immigrants (4.5 percent of state population).[3]

However, unauthorized immigration is hardly relegated to these states or to the American South. In New York, the unauthorized illegal immigration population is estimated to be 650,000 (3.3 percent of state population); in Illinois, it is 475,000 (4.2 percent of the state population); in Maryland, it is 250,000 (4.5 percent of the state population); and in Colorado, it is 210,000 (4.2 percent of the state population). Exhibit 2 below provides additional statistical detail regarding the number of unauthorized immigrants in each of the 50 states and the District of Columbia.

Though illegal population originates from many parts of the world, a handful of nations are responsible for the bulk of illegal migration to America. The Pew Hispanic Center estimates that 60 percent of the unauthorized immigrant

---

3. Pew Research Center, Unauthorized Immigrant Population: National and State Trends, 2010.

Exhibit 2. Share of Unauthorized Immigrants of Total Population by State, 2009

Rank	State	Share	Rank	State	Share
1	California	6.9%	27	Wisconsin	2.2%
2	Nevada	6.8%	28	Arkansas	2.1%
3	Texas	6.5%	29	Idaho	2.1%
4	Arizona	5.8%	30	Iowa	2.1%
5	New Jersey	5.6%	31	Tennessee	2.1%
6	New Mexico	4.9%	32	Indiana	1.9%
7	Maryland	4.5%	33	Minnesota	1.9%
8	Oregon	4.4%	34	Oklahoma	1.7%
9	Georgia	4.3%	35	Mississippi	1.6%
10	Colorado	4.2%	36	Louisiana	1.5%
11	Illinois	4.2%	37	Wyoming	<1.5%
12	Dist. of Columbia	4.1%	38	Michigan	1.4%
13	Utah	3.9%	39	Pennsylvania	1.3%
14	Florida	3.7%	40	Kentucky	1.2%
15	Connecticut	3.3%	41	South Carolina	1.2%
16	New York	3.3%	42	New Hampshire	1.1%
17	North Carolina	3.0%	43	Ohio	1.1%
18	Virginia	3.0%	44	Missouri	1.0%
19	Washington	3.0%	45	Alaska	<1%
20	Alabama	2.8%	46	Montana	<1%
21	Hawaii	2.7%	47	North Dakota	<1%
22	Nebraska	2.6%	48	South Dakota	<1%
23	Rhode Island	2.6%	49	Maine	<0.5%
24	Delaware	2.5%	50	Vermont	<0.5%
25	Massachusetts	2.5%	51	West Virginia	<0.5%
26	Kansas	2.4%			

Source: *Pew Hispanic Center*

population was born in Mexico while another 20 percent was born in other Latin American countries. Exhibit 3 provides detail regarding U.S. unauthorized immigrants by country of birth. According to the federal government, approximately 375,000 illegal immigrants cross the U.S.-Mexico border each year.

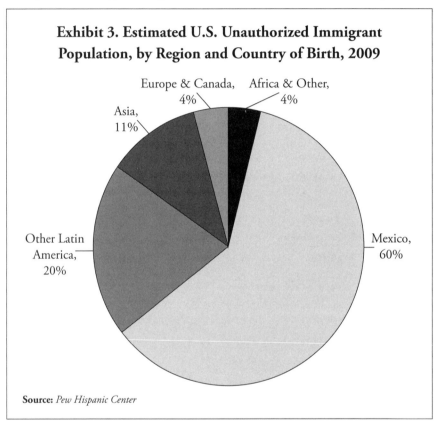

Exhibit 3. Estimated U.S. Unauthorized Immigrant Population, by Region and Country of Birth, 2009

Source: *Pew Hispanic Center*

The unauthorized immigrant population at least doubled in 11 states over the past decade. In Alabama, this population increased more than 400 percent; it surged 350 percent in Mississippi and 225 percent in Louisiana. New York was the sole state to experience a decrease in illegal population (see Exhibit 4).

According to the Pew Hispanic Center, the number of illegal immigrants living in the United States declined over the three-year period ending with March 2010. This is attributed to a weaker economy and tougher enforcement of immigration laws that deterred some fraction of would-be migrants or induced some

Exhibit 4. Unauthorized Immigrant Population Growth by State, 2000–2009

Rank	State	% Change	Rank	State	% Change
1	Alabama	420%	27	Delaware	33%
2	Mississippi	350%	28	Colorado	31%
3	Louisiana	225%	29	North Carolina	31%
4	Iowa	160%	30	Nevada	29%
5	Tennessee	160%	31	Arizona	25%
6	Kentucky	150%	32	Rhode Island	25%
7	Wisconsin	140%	33	Washington	25%
8	Ohio	118%	34	South Carolina	22%
9	Maryland	108%	35	Idaho	20%
10	Arkansas	100%	36	Oklahoma	20%
11	Missouri	100%	37	Kansas	18%
12	Pennsylvania	88%	38	Florida	17%
13	Indiana	85%	39	California	11%
14	Minnesota	73%	40	Illinois	11%
15	New Mexico	73%	41	Massachusetts	7%
16	Georgia	70%	42	Alaska*	0%
17	Utah	69%	43	Dist. of Columbia	0%
18	Virginia	60%	44	Maine*	0%
19	Oregon	55%	45	Montana*	0%
20	Nebraska	50%	46	North Dakota*	0%
21	New Hampshire**	50%	47	South Dakota*	0%
22	Michigan	47%	48	Vermont*	0%
23	Connecticut	47%	49	West Virginia*	0%
24	New Jersey	46%	50	Wyoming*	0%
25	Texas	45%	51	New York	-10%
26	Hawaii	40%			

*In both 2000 and 2009, the state had fewer than 10,000 unauthorized immigrants; **In 2000, the state had fewer than 10,000 unauthorized immigrants.

Source: *Pew Hispanic Center*

to return home. However, with the U.S. economy improving since that time, the negative trend appears to have come to an end.[4] Pew notes that the number of unauthorized immigrants in the nation's workforce, 8 million as of March 2010, did not differ from the Pew Hispanic Center estimate for 2009.[5]

This chapter focuses upon economic and other implications associated with the massive influx of undocumented aliens, with particular focus given to the impact on other minority communities. There are fiscal implications as well, since federal, state, and local government resources are made available to individuals who are not associated with a Social Security number and who frequently pay no income taxes.

ECONOMIC IMPLICATIONS

There are a variety of implications associated with the rapid expansion of undocumented aliens in America. Many of them pertain to the U.S. labor force. The stereotypical notion that undocumented aliens come to America to work appears to be true. Available data from the Pew Hispanic Center indicate that unauthorized immigrants made up 5.2 percent of the civilian labor force in 2010 despite comprising 3.7 percent of the nation's population. It may be because they disproportionately work that many American policy makers have taken a hands-off approach to the issue, apparently adopting what is tantamount to a "What's the harm?" position. As an example of this type of attitude, Congresswoman Debbie Wasserman Schultz (FL), the new head of the Democratic National Committee, recently stated, "The Democrats' position is that we need comprehensive immigration reform. We have 12 million undocumented immigrants in this country that are part of the backbone of our economy. And that is not only a reality but a necessity."

---

4. Pew Research Center, Unauthorized Immigrant Population: National and State Trends, 2010.

5. *Ibid.*

Exhibit 5. Unauthorized Immigrants in U.S. Civilian LaborForce, 2000–2010

Year	Estimated Labor Force (millions)	Share of Labor Force
2010	8.0	5.2%
2009	7.8	5.1%
2008	8.2	5.3%
2007	8.4	5.5%
2006	7.8	5.2%
2005	7.4	5.0%
2004	6.8	4.6%
2003	6.5	4.4%
2002	6.4	4.4%
2001	6.3	4.3%
2000	5.5	3.8%

Source: *Pew Hispanic Center*

EVIDENCE OF LABOR FORCE DISPLACEMENT, PARTICULARLY AMONG OTHER MINORITY GROUPS

A basic understanding of economics provides at least one obvious impact. The arrival of so many illegal immigrants shifts the labor supply curve outward, which implies downward movement in wages and salaries accompanied by higher unemployment as legal residents are displaced.

This displacement is more likely in certain industries. According to the Pew Hispanic Center, undocumented aliens are largely represented in a handful of industries. These include construction, agriculture, leisure and hospitality, services, and manufacturing. Exhibit 6 provides relevant statistical detail.

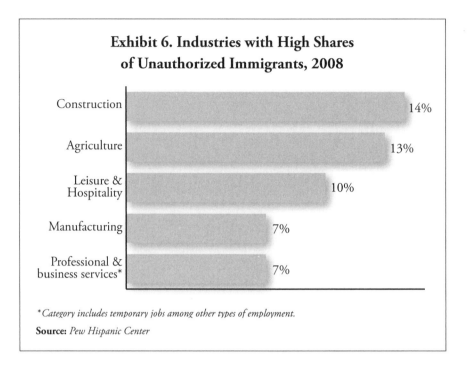

Exhibit 6. Industries with High Shares of Unauthorized Immigrants, 2008

Construction — 14%
Agriculture — 13%
Leisure & Hospitality — 10%
Manufacturing — 7%
Professional & business services* — 7%

Category includes temporary jobs among other types of employment.

Source: *Pew Hispanic Center*

Many commentators have suggested that the jobs occupied by undocumented aliens are those jobs that Americans simply do not want. To the extent that this is true, there is little to no displacement of U.S. citizens in need of employment. For instance, Heidi Shierholz of Economic Policy Institute makes the claim:

> *When considering workers within the same education/experience "class," native-born workers and immigrants are not perfect substitutes. In other words, substituting immigrant workers for native workers who have the same level of education and experience is possible, but limited due to the different characteristics of these two types of workers, including fluency in English. The workers who are the most substitutable for new immigrants are earlier immigrants, so this is the group that ends up shouldering much of the impact of new immigration, rather than native-born workers.*

The data in conjunction with common sense indicate that this is not true. For example, the construction worker unemployment rate as of May 2011 was 16.3 percent according to the Bureau of Labor Statistics. Given a national unemployment rate that remains elevated, it is reasonable to believe that many legal residents of the United States would welcome an opportunity to work in the nation's construction industry, which, among other things, is solidly middle wage. Exhibit 7 provides average hourly wages for the lowest-skilled workers within occupational categories. Note that even the lowest-wage construction occupations easily pay more ($11.86) than the nation's minimum wage, which is currently set at $7.25.

Exhibit 7. Hourly Wages by Occupational Category, July 2009

Occupational Category	Average Hourly Wage*
Management, business, and financial occupations	$18.95
Farming, fishing, and forestry occupations	$9.19
Installation maintenance and repair occupations	$11.44
Transportation and material-moving occupations	$9.98
Production occupations	$9.60
Sales and related occupations	$8.73
Construction and extraction occupations	$11.86
Professional and related occupations	$11.08
Office and administrative support occupations	$10.64
Service occupations	$9.03

Source: *Bureau of Labor Statistics;*

*Average hourly wage for workers with the lowest skill level within each sector.

DISPROPORTIONATE IMPACT UPON AFRICAN AMERICANS

As with many aspects of the American illegal immigration debate, there are two primary competing positions that scholars have adopted with respect to the impact of illegal immigration upon minority groups. One side argues that immigrants merely act as complements to the existing labor force and do not compete for the same jobs. In fact, according to this school of thought, the arrival of illegal immigrants renders native-born workers more prosperous by shifting out the overall demand curve for labor. This line of thought is largely founded on the notion that the immigrant workforce is primarily focused on lower-skilled occupations and that native-born workers retain their opportunity to fill supervisory roles or specialized positions. Moreover, because native-born workers typically enjoy a linguistic advantage over immigrants, it is more likely that newly arriving undocumented serve as substitutes to earlier immigrants as opposed to native-born workers. As we shall see, this school of thought largely revolves around area studies.

The competing position is that immigrants serve as substitutes to the native-born workforce, particularly in lower-wage categories. These scholars emphasize that the increase in low-skilled labor supply disproportionately impacts African Americans, who are characterized by less educational attainment and income than the balance of the United States. This argument is summarized in the graphic below, with the labor supply curve pushed to the right by the influx of competing workers. The end result is lower wages and likely greater unemployment among competing native-born workers. This school of thought largely relies upon national-level studies.

COMPARING THE AREA AND NATIONAL APPROACHES

One of the most influential area approach studies was David Card's 1990 study regarding the impact of the Mariel boatlift on the African American workforce in Miami.[6] Over a short period of time, the size of Miami's labor force surged 7 percent. The study determined that there was little impact to the wages and employment opportunities for Miami's African American population. This conclusion was reached by comparing the state of the economy in Miami to that of comparable cities that did not experience an influx of immigration. Between 1979 and 1981, the black unemployment rate in Miami rose from 8.3 to 9.6 percent, a 1.3-percentage-point increase. During that same period, the unemployment rate in other cities collectively rose from 10.3 to 12.6 percent, a 2.3-percentage-point increase.

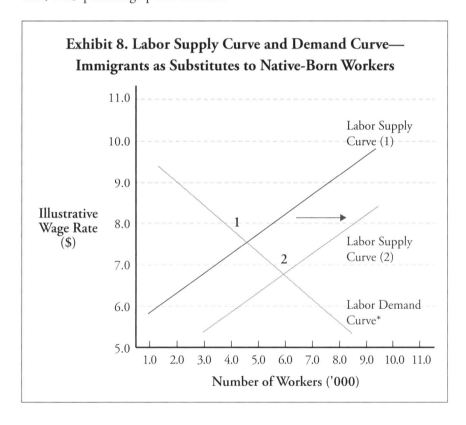

Exhibit 8. Labor Supply Curve and Demand Curve— Immigrants as Substitutes to Native-Born Workers

---

6. David Card, "The Impact of the Mariel Boatlift on the Miami Labor Market," *Industrial and Labor Relations Review* 43 (January 1990): 245–257.

Card's (1990) study results raise at least two analytical questions, according to George Borjas of Harvard University: "Why is the evidence so different from the typical presumption in the debate over immigration policy and why does the evidence seem to be so inconsistent with the implications of the simplest supply-demand equilibrium model?"[7]

According to Borjas, the "entry of immigrants into the local labor market may well lower the wage of competing workers and increase the wage of complementary workers initially. Over time, however, natives will likely respond to immigration. After all, it is not in the best interest of native-owned firms or native workers to sit idly by and watch immigrants change economic opportunities. All natives now have incentives to change their behavior in ways that take advantage of the altered economic landscape."[8]

It is likely that the most mobile workers would be those native-born workers that are close substitutes for new immigrants, particularly those in lower-skilled occupations. These negatively impacted native-born workers can and do respond by moving to other cities where higher levels of undocumented immigration did not transpire. The overall effect in the two cities is likely an increase in labor supply and thus a decrease in wages. As Borjas indicates, "in the end, all workers who compete with immigrants, regardless of where they live, are worse off because there are now many more such workers." Therefore, as long as workers and firms respond to the entry of immigrants by "voting with their feet," there is little reason to expect a correlation between the earnings of native workers in particular cities and the presence of immigrants. In short, the comparison of local labor markets may be hiding the true "macro" impact of immigration.

Having observed that employers are more likely to view workers with the same levels of education and experience as substitutes for one another, Borjas defines skill groups along these two dimensions (Borjas, 2006). Not surprisingly,

---

7. Borjas, G.J, (2005), *Labor Economics* (Third Edition), New York, NY: McGraw-Hill/Irwin, Page 186.

8. *Ibid.*

he finds substantial variation in immigrants' share of employment in education-experience categories. Findings for the years 1960–2000 enabled him to estimate impacts on the average weekly earnings of 32 groups of men—from high school dropouts with less than six years of potential work experience to college graduates with more than 35 years of experience.

He finds that a 10 percent increase in the number of workers in an education-experience category would reduce the average weekly earnings of men in that group by approximately 4 percent before secondary adjustments in capital formation or investments in skills by workers are made. Using a simulation of the impact of large numbers of immigrants analogous to the change in the number of foreign-born male workers between 1980 and 2000, Borjas calculated that the average weekly earnings of native-born men as a group would be reduced by 3 to 4 percent, with high school dropouts experiencing the largest adverse impacts. He estimated that their earnings would be about 9 percent lower than they would be in the absence of increased competition from foreign-born workers.

In a 2007 study based on U.S. Census data from 1960 to 2000, Borjas finds that "a 10-percent immigrant-induced increase in the supply of a particular skill group is associated with a reduction in the African-American wage of 4.0 percent, a reduction in the black employment rate of 3.5 percentage points, and an increase in the black institutionalization rate of 0.8 percent."[9] The study goes on to suggest that the impact is somewhat different upon white men, with a 10 percent increase in immigrant labor supply associated with reduced wages of 4.1 percent but a reduction in the employment rate of 1.6 percent.[10]

If one were to apply Borjas's (2007) parameters to the broader U.S. economy, the increase in undocumented alien workforce would have produced a 16 percent reduction in African American wages and a 15 percent decline

---

9. Borjas et al., "Immigration and African-American Employment Opportunities: The Response of Wages, Employment, and Incarceration to Labor Supply Shocks," *NBER Working Paper 12518*, National Bureau of Economic Research, September 2006, Page 4. http://www.nber.org/papers/w12518

10. Ibid.

in the black employment rate. In more concrete terms, in 2009 the average annual income for blacks with less than a high school diploma was $18,046. According to the Bureau of Labor Statistics, employment among blacks with less than a high school diploma totaled 1,096,000. Again, based upon Borjas's estimated parameters, had the flood of illegal immigrants not occurred, it is estimated that African Americans with less than a high school diploma would have earned roughly $21,000 on average in 2009, with 116,100 more African Americans working that year ceteris paribus.

This translates into African America wage income loss of $3.2 billion. That income would have supported nearly 45,000 additional jobs, many of them in communities with high proportions of African Americans. These 45,000 jobs would have been associated with another $2.2 billion in income. Exhibit 9 provides summary detail of this portion of the analysis.

Exhibit 9. Annual Economic Impact of Increased Wages by U.S. African American Workers with Less than a High School Education

Type of Impact	Value
Direct Lost Income ($millions)	$3,238
Lost Jobs	$44,957
Lost Labor Income ($millions)	$2,190
Lost Business Sales ($millions)	$7,321

Source: *Sage Policy Group, Inc.*

This lost employment and income translate into foregone government income. Were the incomes of African Americans lacking a high school degree not artificially devalued by the influx of undocumented labor, state and local governments around the nation would have collected more than $444 million in annual income in 2009, and federal government coffers would have been enriched by more than $500 million.

Of course, these are not large numbers in the context of overall government budgets. However, there are other fiscal implications, including the need for government to provide additional unemployment benefits to displaced workers, invest in ongoing retraining programs, spend more on welfare/food stamps, and at least potentially expend more upon public safety. The cost of these expenditures could be in the billions of dollars.

Exhibit 10. Annual Fiscal Impact of Increased Wages by U.S. African American Workers with Less than a High School Education

State and Local	Value ($millions)
Dividends	$32
Social Insurance Tax	$5
Sales Tax	$139
Property Tax	$130
Income Tax	$47
Corporate Profits Tax	$16
Other Taxes and Fees	$75
Total State and Local	**$444**

Federal	Value ($millions)
Social Insurance Tax	$230
Excise Taxes	$20
Custom Duty	$9
Federal Nontaxes	$15
Corporate Profits	$65
Income Tax	$171
Total Federal	**$509**

The impact upon the demand for government services is reasonably apparent in budgetary data, including data pertaining to communities with large proportions of potentially dislocated African Americans. Not coincidentally, many of these states are also among the states with the largest increases in undocumented population since 2000.

For instance, in Louisiana, spending on public assistance expanded 240 percent between 2000 and 2010, a period during which the undocumented population grew more than 200 percent (third most rapid pace of unauthorized immigrant population growth in the nation). Similarly, spending on public assistance jumped 148 percent in Ohio while spending in the general fund inched up just 25 percent. Undocumented population expanded more than 100 percent during this period, ranking Ohio eighth along this dimension. Similar trends are apparent in Tennessee and Arkansas, where public assistance spending rose 108 and 75 percent, respectively. With respect to percentage of undocumented population growth, Tennessee ranked fifth in the nation over the past decade and Arkansas tenth.

NATIONAL APPROACH LIMITATIONS

Although the use of national data should overcome the most significant drawbacks associated with the area approach, the nationwide approach also has limitations. In particular, it does not account for the secondary adjustments that are likely to occur as undocumented population expands. Consequently, it may overstate the long-run impact of immigration on native workers' earnings if the presence of foreign-born workers stimulates demand for additional workers by attracting more capital to an area or industry.

Borjas himself noted the potential importance of such adjustments in a recent paper that estimated the long-run impact of immigration on the earnings of native workers if the nation's capital stock increased by enough to keep the returns on capital constant. Borjas found that if complete adjustment of the capital stock occurred, there would be no long-run impact on the average weekly earnings of native men overall. In that circumstance, some groups would gain while others would lose. The workers most likely to lose would be those whose education and experience most closely resembled those of the new immigrants. In particular, Borjas estimated that the earnings of men without a high school diploma would be reduced by the influx of immigrants. Whether the nation's capital stock would adjust to the expansion of the immigrant workforce to the extent used in that illustration is not known, but it is seems reasonable to believe that some level of adjustment would occur given that labor and capital are complements.

Likewise, it is reasonable to presume that some natives would stay in school longer as a consequence of the influx of large numbers of foreign-born workers who lack a high school education. Attaining a diploma represents one way of avoiding direct competition with new arrivals, though it is unclear how relevant this is for adults who lack a high school degree. How much educational attainment responds to an influx of undocumented aliens is unclear, but to the extent that it occurs, Borjas's original estimates of negative impact upon black male and other wages are likely overstated.

Destruction of Future American Potential

The large-scale entry of undocumented aliens may help explain the incredibly high rates of teenage unemployment plaguing America. After all, teenagers and illegal aliens are often associated with a lack of significant educational attainment and experience. Correspondingly, they represent natural competitors in the U.S. labor market.

According to the Bureau of Labor Statistics, the average teenage unemployment rate in the United States for 2010 was 25.8 percent, by far the highest rate of the past decade. The Center for Immigration Studies found that, on average, a 10 percent increase in the immigrant share of a state's workforce from 1994 to 2007 reduced the labor force participation rate of U.S.-born teenagers by 7.9 percent. Moreover, they found that in the summer of 2007, one in five workers was an immigrant in precisely those occupations that employ the most teenagers. The report also reveals that between 1994 and 2007, immigrants registered substantial job gains in those occupations in which teenage employment declined the most.[11]

Though teenage unemployment is clearly linked to the business cycle, it has exploded since the year 2000 due both to greater competition for work and to recent economic weakness. The loss of employment opportunities among this group has significant economic consequences, in the form of greater difficulty building skills, more problematic identification of career paths and preferences, weaker labor force attachment, and poor work habits. Those who do not work as teenagers earn less and work less often later in life, particularly those who do not attain additional education after high school.[12]

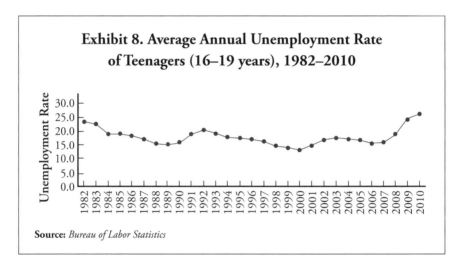

Exhibit 8. Average Annual Unemployment Rate of Teenagers (16–19 years), 1982–2010

Source: *Bureau of Labor Statistics*

The teenage unemployment rate is particularly high among minorities. As of May 2011, the African American teenage unemployment rate stood at 40.7 percent. The Asian teenage unemployment rate stood at 38.3 percent. White teenage unemployment was much lower at 20.7 percent.[13] The very strong implication

11.   Camarota, Steven A., and Jensenius, Karen (2010), A Drought of Summer Jobs: Immigration and the Long-Term Decline in Employment Among U.S. Born Teenagers.

12.   *Ibid.*

13.   BLS, Current Population Survey, available at http://www.bls.gov/cps/.

is that less experienced, lower-skilled teenagers are more likely to be displaced by undocumented aliens than other demographic groups. This may have much to do with co-location, since undocumented aliens are more likely to inhabit communities that are disproportionately minority and low income.

Data from the Bureau of Labor Statistics indicate that minority unemployment is higher in precisely those markets that are most closely associated with the arrival of large numbers of illegal aliens. For example, as referenced above, the state with the largest number of undocumented aliens in the United States is California. The African American unemployment rate in California in 2009 was 14.3 percent. By contrast, West Virginia, which is associated with a far smaller number of illegal aliens, was associated with an African American unemployment rate of 8.4 percent.[14]

The relationship between illegal immigration and high rates of minority unemployment is an intuitive one. Minorities disproportionately occupy lower-wage, lower-skilled positions that require less formal education. For instance, the Bureau of Labor Statistics reports that 37.9 percent of whites work in management, professional, and related occupations, compared with 29.1 percent of African Americans. Additionally, 25.1 percent of African Americans held service jobs in 2010 as opposed to 16.6 percent of whites. Exhibit 9 provides relevant statistical detail.

Correspondingly, minorities are more likely to be displaced by the army of lower-skilled undocumented workers, and that is precisely what has occurred. In 1992, the gap between white and African American unemployment was 4.5 percent. Today, it is 7.3 percent.[15] Exhibit 10 shows the average annual unemployment rates of African American and white workers since 2001. Though there are a number of other factors that have undoubtedly impacted African American unemployment rates, competition with illegal labor appears to be one of the most important.

14.　BLS, Local Area Unemployment Statistics, available at http://www.bls.gov/lau/.

15.　BLS, Current Population Survey.

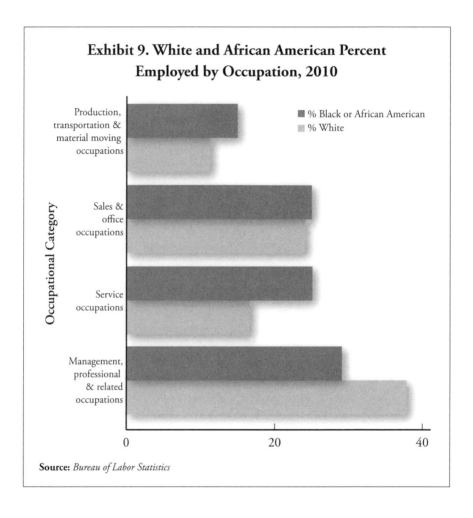

Exhibit 9. White and African American Percent Employed by Occupation, 2010

Source: *Bureau of Labor Statistics*

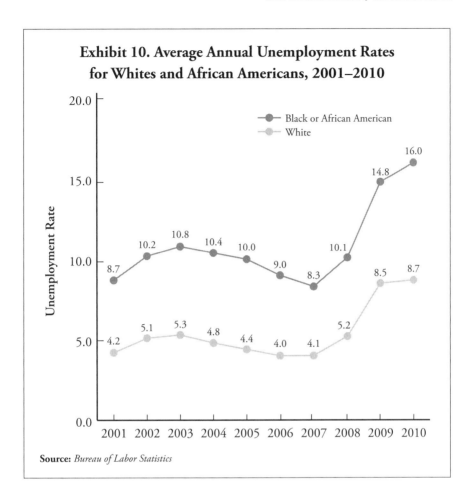

Exhibit 10. Average Annual Unemployment Rates for Whites and African Americans, 2001–2010

Source: *Bureau of Labor Statistics*

A Simple Analytical Exercise

To provide readers with a sense of just how impactful illegal immigration is, the authors of this report conducted a simple data-driven experiment. The Bureau of Labor Statistics measures unemployment in a number of different ways. The most prominent measure is called U3, which measures the percentage of the civilian labor force that is not employed. A somewhat broader measure of unemployment is U4, which, in addition to U3, includes discouraged workers (those who would like to have a job but have given up looking for one).

In 2010, there were 7.2 million unauthorized immigrants working in the United States (8 million in the labor force, of which roughly 10 percent were unemployed). If one assumes that, at the extreme, these jobs would be filled by legal residents if they were not filled by undocumented workers, the U4 unemployment rate in 2010 nationally would have been just 5.6 percent as opposed to 10.3 percent. While it is quite likely that many of these jobs would go unfilled by legal residents because of an unwillingness to work at lower wages, this simple analysis provides a sense of just how much potential labor market dislocation is associated with the rapid expansion of the nation's undocumented alien population.

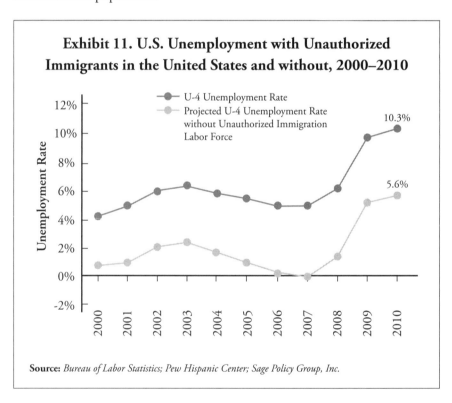

Exhibit 11. U.S. Unemployment with Unauthorized Immigrants in the United States and without, 2000–2010

Source: *Bureau of Labor Statistics; Pew Hispanic Center; Sage Policy Group, Inc.*

EXPORTING MONEY

Not only is the income earned by undocumented aliens frequently at the expense of legal residents but also earnings are often literally sent out of the country. The Inter-American Development Bank estimated that Latino immigrants repatriated about $42 billion in 2009 to other nations. This has the effect of shrinking the U.S. economy as money that would otherwise be circulated through local retailers, service providers, local governments, and others is simply jettisoned abroad. This results in a multitude of negative economic impacts, including reduced government service provision, fewer jobs, and less activity among small U.S. businesses.

FISCAL IMPLICATIONS

In addition to a variety of economic implications are fiscal implications. Broadly, these implications are attributable to two phenomena: (1) unpaid taxes and (2) augmented utilization of government services.

The Pew Hispanic Center estimates that undocumented aliens living in the United States for fewer than 10 years earned $35,000 in median household income as of 2007. Though some of this income translates into retail sales taxes paid and perhaps other forms of tax collection, these earnings largely go untaxed. The Urban Institute found that in 1998, unauthorized immigrants in New York State paid an average of 15 percent of their income in federal, state, and local taxes, while other immigrant groups paid between 21 and 31 percent.[16] When U.S. states and municipalities were flush with cash several fiscal years ago, this may have been simpler to ignore. But with virtually all states in the union now facing significant structural shortfalls, the deflection of

---

16. The Impact of Unauthorized Immigrants on the Budgets of State and Local Governments. Congressional Budget Office. December 2007. Page 2; See Jeffrey S. Passel, *Unauthorized Migrants: Numbers and Characteristics* (background briefing prepared for the Task Force on Immigration and America's Future, Washington, D.C., Pew Hispanic Center, June 14, 2005), available at http://pewhispanic.org/files/reoirts/46.pdf.

income to those who generally do not pay taxes has become more difficult to simply shrug off.

The demand for local government services easily outstrips the taxes that are paid by undocumented aliens. A 2007 study by the Congressional Budget Office (CBO) noted that the costs of services to state and local governments associated with illegal immigration are disproportionately higher than those of federal agencies.[17] While unauthorized immigrants are prohibited from receiving Social Security and certain need-based programs such as Medicaid (other than emergency services), food stamps, and Temporary Assistance for Needy Families, state and local governments bear the burden of providing services related to education, health care, and law enforcement to individuals residing in their jurisdictions.[18]

The CBO study noted that these costs are higher than they otherwise would be because most undocumented immigrants are uninsured, thereby increasing local government financial burdens for the use of emergency response services and public hospitals.[19] Additionally, the costs of educating students who do not speak English fluently are 20 percent to 40 percent higher than the costs incurred for native-born students.[20] In certain California jurisdictions, spending on unauthorized immigrants by local governments ranged between 5 and 10 percent of total spending for those services.[21]

---

17. The Impact of Unauthorized Immigrants on the Budgets of State and Local Governments. Congressional Budget Office. December 2007. Page 1.

18. *Ibid.*

19. *Ibid.* See Dana P. Goldman, James P. Smith, and Neeraj Sood, "Legal Status and Health Insurance among Immigrants," *Health Affairs*, vol. 24, no 6 (2005), pp. 1640–1653, available at http://content.healthaffairs.org/cgi/reprint/24/6/1640.

20. *bid* at p. 2.; See Jose Cardenas and others, *Bilingual Cost Analysis* (San Antonio: Intercultural Development Research Association, 1976).; See also Albert Cortez, *Insufficient Funding for Bilingual Education in Texas*, IDRA Newsletter (San Antonio: Intercultural Development Research Association, 2004).

21. *Ibid.* at p. 3.

A 1982 Supreme Court decision ruled that states may not exclude children from public education because of their immigration status.[22] Over time, the fiscal impact of this decision has been substantial. The CBO estimates that children who are unauthorized immigrants represent almost 4 percent of the overall school-age population nationally.[23] Importantly, the nonpartisan Congressional Budget Office concludes that tax revenues generated by unauthorized immigrants do not offset the costs of education, health care, and law enforcement.

On the basis of a population estimate generated by the Pew Hispanic Center, analysts at the New Mexico Fiscal Policy Project report that for the 2003–2004 school year, total spending in New Mexico at the state and local levels for 9,200 unauthorized immigrant schoolchildren was approximately $67 million.[24] Costs are likely to have increased significantly since that period. Of the estimated 40,000 unauthorized immigrants presently residing in New Mexico, 95 percent are believed to be recent arrivals, having lived in the state for fewer than 10 years.[25]

The Iowa Legislative Services Agency reported that the estimated 70,000 unauthorized immigrants in that state paid between $45.5 million and $70.9 million state income and sales taxes in fiscal year 2004. Based upon total spending from the state's general fund and the number of state residents, the agency estimated the cost for providing all services to unauthorized immigrants was $107.4 million in FY2004.[26]

Similarly, recent estimates indicate that annual costs for unauthorized immigrants in Colorado were between $217 million and $225 million for corrections, education, and Medicaid. By comparison, taxes collected from

---

22. *Plyer v. Doe*, 457 U.S. 202 (1982).

23. The Impact of Unauthorized Immigrants on the Budgets of State and Local Governments. Congressional Budget Office. December 2007, p. 8.

24. *Ibid.*

25. *Ibid.*

26. *Ibid.* at p. 10.

unauthorized immigrants at both the state and local levels are estimated at between $159 million and $194 million annually.[27]

A report prepared by the state comptroller of Texas estimated that in 2006, the state collected $424 million more in revenue from unauthorized immigrants than it spent to provide education, health care, and law enforcement for that population. However, the state also estimated that local governments incurred $1.4 billion in uncompensated costs for health care and law enforcement.

In recent years, the federal government has established several programs to assist state and local governments in funding the additional costs associated with providing services to unauthorized immigrants. While this offers temporary relief to state and local government budgets, these programs ultimately either contribute to the national debt or are passed on to federal taxpayers.[28]

CONCLUSION

This analysis provides data and qualitative information from a variety of sources to suggest that the economic dislocation associated with America's 11 million undocumented aliens is massive. The emergence of this population has:

- Increased unemployment, particularly among minorities and teenagers;
- Resulted in larger fiscal gaps among state and local governments;
- Led to the loss of $42 billion in repatriated funds each year, largely headed to Latin American nations;
- Disproportionately impacted legal residents who seek employment in a number of industries, including construction and leisure/hospitality; and
- Created a public policy dilemma regarding what to do next.

---

27. Baker and Jones (2006). State and Local Taxes Paid in Colorado by Undocumented Immigrants.
28. Op. cit., CBO, p. 10.

One of the most serious issues is that a growing number of children of undocumented aliens are being born in the United States. This makes deportation or other forms of legal redress far more complicated. The number of children born to at least one unauthorized-immigrant parent in 2009 was 350,000, comprising 8 percent of all U.S. births. An analysis of the year of entry of unauthorized immigrants who became parents in 2009 indicates that 61 percent arrived in America before 2004, 30 percent arrived between 2004 and 2007, and 9 percent arrived between 2008 and 2010.

In other words, the issue of undocumented aliens continues to mushroom in America. Based on current patterns, teenage unemployment among legal residents will continue to skyrocket, the unemployment rate gap between African Americans and other Americans will continue to climb, and the fiscal strains caused by the provision of law enforcement services, health care, and education to undocumented aliens will expand further.

Unfortunately, the ideological gaps between policy makers in Washington, D.C., strongly suggest that no offsetting policies are likely to be implemented, which means that current trajectories will simply continue. Presuming that the U.S. economy continues to recover, the pace of illegal immigration into the United States is likely to reaccelerate while the federal policy-making community remains idle.

Appendix

Notes

Chapter 1: A Tarnished Golden Door

— Kochar, Dr. Rakesh. "After the Great Recession: Foreign-Born Gain Jobs; Native-Born Lose Jobs." Pew Hispanic Center, 2010. http://www.pewhispanic.org.

— Camarota, Steven A., and Jensenius, Karen. "A Detailed Look at Immigrant Employment by Occupation." Center for Immigration Studies, August 2009. http://www.cis.org.

— Corwin, Ronald G. "How Immigration Is Impacting the U.S. Social Economy." http://www.socialissues.us.

— Annual Population Growth. Center for Immigration Studies. http://www.cis.org.

— Sobhani, Rob. "United? States: Our Immigration Problem." *National Review* online, July 9, 2002.

— Hakimzaluh, Shirin. "Iran: A Vast Diaspora Abroad and Millions of Refugees at Home." Migration Information Service, September 2006.

— Harrison, Frances. "Huge Cost of Iranian Brain Drain." BBC News, January 8, 2007.

— "Billions of Dollars of Oil Money Diverted into Regime Coffers." Iranbriefing.net, February 28, 2011.

Chapter 2: The Cost of Immigration

— Beck, Roy. "Immigration Gumball Theory." http://www.youtube.com, updated 2010.

— Krikorian, Mark. "Legal Good/Illegal Bad?" *National Review* online, June 1, 2007.

— Graham, Otis. "What's Wrong with US Immigration Policy?" Volume 16, Number 4 (Summer 2006), for the Brookings Institution.

— "Between Two Worlds: How Young Latinos Come of Age in America." Pew Hispanic Center, December 11, 2009. http://www.pewhispanic.org.

— Camarota, Steven A. "Welfare Use by Immigrant Households with Children: A Look at Cash, Medicaid, Housing, and Food Programs." Center for Immigration Studies, April 2011. http://www.cis.org.

— Telles, Edward E., and Ortiz, Vilma. *Generations of Exclusion: Mexican Americans, Assimilation and Race.* Russell Sage Foundation, 2008.

— Corwin, Ronald G. "How Immigration Is Impacting the U.S. Social Economy." http://www.socialissues.us.

— Tomas Rivera Policy Institute. http://www.trpi.org.

— Kochar, Dr. Rakesh. "After the Great Recession: Foreign-Born Gain Jobs; Native-Born Lose Jobs." Pew Hispanic Center, 2010. http://www.pewhispanic.org.

— "Unauthorized Immigrant Population: National and State Trends." Pew Hispanic Center. http://www.pewhispanic.org.

— "The High Cost of Cheap Labor: Illegal Immigrants and the Federal Budget." Center for Immigration Studies. http://www.cis.org.

— Vedantem, Vandar. "Foreign-Born Workers Gained Jobs, While Native-Born Lost Them." *The Washington Post*, October 30, 2010.

— WeHireAliens.com

— Fraudulent Social Security Cards. Center for Immigration Studies. http://www.cis.org.

— Marcelo M. Suarez-Orozo, Immigration Research Center at NYU.

— Mazzoli, Romano L., and Simpson, Alan K. "Enacting Immigration Reform, Again." *The Washington Post*, September 15, 2006.

— Rector, Robert. "Amnesty Lost: White House Report Hides the Real Costs of Amnesty and Low Skill Immigration." Heritage Foundation, June 26, 2007.

— DREAM Act. Center for Immigration Studies. http://www.cis.org.

Chapter 3: A Tale of Two Cities

— San Diego Association of Governments Data on Border Crossings. http://www.sandag.org.

— Navarro, Tania. "Tijuana and San Diego Not Really One Region, Study Says." SDNN, February 17, 2010.

— International Community Foundation. *Blurred Borders: Transboundary Issues and Solutions in the San Diego/Tijuana Border Region*. 2004. http://www.icfdn.org/publications/blurredborders/index.htm.

— Cruz, Teddy. "A City Made of Waste." *The Nation*, February 16, 2009.

— Martinez, Oscar J. *U.S.-Mexico Borderlands: Historical and Contemporary Perspectives*. Wilmington: Jaguar Books on Latin America, 1996.

— Archibold, Randal C. "Massacre in Tijuana Recalls Worst Era." *The New York Times*, October 25, 2010.

— Mexico ranks fourth among top petroleum producers in the world. The top 10 are: 1. Saudi Arabia, 2. Russia, 3. Iran, 4. Mexico, 5. China, 6. Norway, 7. Canada, 8. Venezuela, 9. United Arab Emirates, 10. Kuwait.

— Weiner, Tim. "Corruption and Waste Bleed Mexico's Oil Lifeline." *The New York Times*, January 21, 2003.

— The U.S. Attorneys Annual Statistical Report for Fiscal Year 2009. http://www.justice.gov/usao/reading_room/reports/asr2009/statrpt.pdf.

— National Drug Intelligence Center. "National Drug Threat Assessment 2009." http://www.justice.gov/ndic/pubs31/31379/index.htm.

— O'Grady, Mary Anastasia. "Can Mexico Be Saved?" *The Wall Street Journal*, November 13, 2010.

— Coughlin, Thomas. "Border Relations with Mexico Complicated by High Crime Rates." *University of San Diego Vista*, updated October 2, 2010. http://www.theusdvista.com.

— Morris, Stephen D. "Corruption and Mexican Political Culture." *Journal of the Southwest*, December 22, 2003.

— Ody, Elizabeth. "Carlos Slim Tops Forbes List of Billionaires for Second Year." *Bloomberg*, March 10, 2011.

— Caruso-Cabrera, Michelle. "Carlos Slim Won't Give Away His Fortune Like Buffett and Gates." CNBC, January 20, 2011.

Chapter 4: Blacks Left Behind

— Guzzardi, Joe. "Why the Black Caucus Looks the Other Way on Immigration." http://www.VDARE.com, May 2010.

— Fair, T. Willard. "Amnesty for illegal workers is not just a slap in the face to black Americans. It's an economic disaster." Ad sponsored by the Coalition for the Future American Worker, 2010.

— Analysis of CBC Stands on Immigration: U.S. Border Control Report. http://www.usbc.org.

— Riley, Jason L. "The NAACP's Unhealthy Tea Party Obsession." *The Wall Street Journal*, October 25, 2010.

— Children's Defense Fund 2010 Report. http://www.childrensdefense.org.

— Alexander, Ames, and Ordonez, Franco. "More than 300 Arrested in S.C. Raid at Poultry Plant." *Charlotte Observer*, October 8, 2008.

— Malanga, Steven. "The Rainbow Coalition Evaporates." *City Journal*, Winter 2008.

— Newman, Katherine, and Lennon, Chauncy. "The Job Ghetto." *The American Prospect*, June 23, 1995. http://www.prospect.org.

— Government Accounting Office Report on Los Angeles Janitorial Services. http://www.gao.gov.

— Pager, Devah, and Western, Bruce. "Discrimination in Low-Wage Labor Markets: Evidence from an Experimental Audit Study in New York City." Princeton University, 2005.

— Harvest Institute Reports. http://www.harvestinstitute.org.

— Hutchinson, Earl Ofari. "The Black-Latino Blame Game." *Los Angeles Times*, November 25, 2007.

— Hutchinson, Earl Ofari. *The Hutchinson Political Report.* http://www.earlofarihutchinson.blogspot.com.

Chapter 5: Population Insanity

— United States Census, 2010.

— "The Law of Large Numbers." *The Economist*, September 11, 2010.

— Camarota, Steven A. "100 Million More: Projecting the Impact of Immigration on the U.S. Population 2007 to 2060." Center for Immigration Studies, August 2007. http://www.cis.org.

— Beck, Roy, and Kolankiewicz, Leon. "Forsaking Fundamentals: The Environmental Establishment Abandons U.S. Population Stabilization." Center for Immigration Studies, March 2001. http://www.cis.org.

— McKinley, James, Jr. "Population 'Tipping Point' in Texas, as Hispanics Get Closer to Parity with Whites." *The New York Times*, February 17, 2011.

— Somashekhar, Sandhya. "Activists Seek to Increase Hispanics' Clout." *The Washington Post*, March 26, 2011.

— Bauerlein, Valerie. "Population Jumps in North Carolina." *The Wall Street Journal*, March 3, 2011.

— Gioia, Vincent. "Are Children Born of Illegal Immigrants U.S. Citizens?" http://FamilySecurityMatters.org.

— Eastman, John C. "Born in the USA: Does That Guarantee Citizenship?" *Des Moines Register*, September 16, 2007.

— Wood, Charles. "Losing Control of America's Future: The Census, Birthright Citizenship and Illegal Aliens." *Harvard Journal of Law and Public Policy*, Spring 1999.

— "Nations Granting Birthright Citizenship." NumbersUSA. http://www.numbersusa.org.

— Richburg, Keith B. "For Many Pregnant Chinese, a U.S. Passport for Baby Remains a Powerful Lure." *The Washington Post*, July 18, 2010.

— Feere, Jon. "Birthright Citizenship in the United States: A Global Comparison." Center for Immigration Studies. http://www.cis.org.

— Kolankiewicz, Leon, and Camarota, Steven A. "Immigration to the United States and Worldwide Greenhouse Gas Emissions." Center for Immigration Studies, September 2008. http://www.cis.org.

Chapter 6: The Assimilation Fallacy

— Tyrell, R. Emmett, Jr. "Multiculturalism Has Failed." *The Washington Times*, February 16, 2011.

— Renshon, Stanley. "Becoming American: The Hidden Core of the Immigration Debate." *FrontPage Magazine*, February 28, 2007.

— Fonte, John. "Dual Allegiance: A Challenge to Immigration Reform and Patriotic Assimilation." Center for Immigration Studies, November 2005. http://www.cis.org.

— Malkin, Michelle. "Immigration and National Security." *Imprints*, July 2008.

— Schulte, Bret. "Mexican Immigrants Prove Slow to Fit In." *U.S. News & World Report*, May 15, 2008.

Chapter 7: A Call for Leadership

— Robinson, Peter. "Immigration: What Would Reagan Do?" Wall Street Journal online, June 15, 2010.

— Theodore Roosevelt's 1894 speech on immigration. http://www.theodore-roosevelt.com.

Chapter 8: Step One—End Linguistic Welfare

— McAlpin, K. C. "Foreign Language Driver's Tests Threaten Public Safety." *US-English*, July 26, 2005. http://www.us-english.org.

— Krauthammer, Charles. "In Plain English: Let's Make It Official." *Time*, June 4, 2006.

— McAlpin, K. C. "English: Why It's Time to Make It Official." *US-English*, July 26, 2005. http://www.us-english.org.

— Cannava, Jayne. "Make English the Official Language." *ProEnglish*, September 24, 2010. http://www.proenglish.org.

Chapter 9: Step Two—Enforce the Laws on the Books

— Statement of Mark Krikorian, executive director, Center for Immigration Studies, before the Committee on the Judiciary, Subcommittee on Immigration Policy and Enforcement, January 26, 2011.

— Camarota, Steven. "From Bad to Worse: Unemployment and Underemployment Among Less-Educated U.S.-Born Workers, 2007 to 2010." Center for Immigration Studies, August 2010. http://www.cis.org.

— Camarota, Steven. "Immigration and Economic Stagnation: An Examination of Trends 2000 to 2010." Center for Immigration Studies, November 2010. http://www.cis.org.

— Stoddard, Ed. "Exclusive: Over a Million Immigrants Land U.S. jobs in 2008–10." Reuters, January 20, 2011. http://www.reuters.com/article/idUSTRE70J37P20110120.

— Kammer, Jerry. "Immigration Raids at Smithfield: How an ICE Enforcement Action Boosted Union Organizing and the Employment of American Workers." Center for Immigration Studies, July 2009. http://www.cis.org.

— Greenhouse, Steven. "After 15 Years, North Carolina Plant Unionizes." *The New York Times*, December 12, 2008. http://www.nytimes.com/2008/12/13/us/13smithfield.html.

— Kammer, Jerry. "The 2006 Swift Raids: Assessing the Impact of Immigration Enforcement Actions at Six Facilities." Center for Immigration Studies, March 2009. http://cis.org/2006SwiftRaids.

— Mortenson, Ronald W., PhD. "Illegal but Not Undocumented: Identity Theft, Document Fraud and Illegal Employment." Center for Immigration Studies, June 2009. http://www.cis.org.

— Preston, Julia, and Semple, Kirk. "U.S. Hardens Its Stance on an Immigrant Policy." *The New York Times*, February 18, 2011.

— Tavernise, Sabrina. "Caught Unawares by an Anti-Immigrant Mood." *The New York Times*, February 18, 2011.

— Kephart, Janice. "REAL ID Implementation: Less Expensive, Doable, and Helpful in Reducing Fraud." Center for Immigration Studies, January 2011. http://www.cis.org.

— ibid. "Real ID Implementation Embraced by 41 States; Driver's Licenses Still at Risk of Terrorist Abuse." Center for Immigration Studies, April 2011. http://www.cis.org.

— Camarota, Steven, and Jensenius, Karen. "A Shifting Tide: Recent Trends in the Illegal Immigrant Population." Center for Immigration Studies, July 2009. http://www.cis.org.

— "UA to Co-Lead DHS Center for Border Security and Immigration." *University Communications*, February 26, 2008.

— Vaughan, Jessica. "Secure Communities, Please." *Numbers USA*, March 14, 2011.

Chapter 10: Step Three—A Five-Year Immigration Moratorium

— Seminara, David. "No Coyote Needed: U.S. Visas Still an Easy Ticket in Developing Countries." Center for Immigration Studies, March 2008. http://www.cis.org.

— Vaughan, Jessica. "Modernizing America's Welcome Mat: The Implementation of US-VISIT." Center for Immigration Studies, August 2005. http://www.cis.org.

— Monger, Randall, and Barr, Macreadie. "Nonimmigrant Admissions to the United States: 2009." DHS Office of Immigration Statistics Annual Flow Report, April 2009.

— Grieco, Elizabeth M. "Length of Visit of Non-immigrants Departing the United States in 2003." Department of Homeland Security, Office of Immigration Statistics, March 2005.

— Kephart, Janice. "Amending the Immigration and Naturalization Act to Eliminate the Diversity Visa Lottery Immigrant Program." Testimony before the House Committee on the Judiciary, Subcommittee on Immigration Policy and Enforcement, April 2011.

— "U.S. Not Racing Visa Overstays." NumbersUSA, October 12, 2009.

Chapter 11: Step Four—End Family Reunification

— Reasoner, W. D. "Birthright Citizenship for the Children of Visitors: A National Security Problem in the Making?" Center for Immigration Studies, March 2011. http://www.cis.org.

— Feere, Jon. "Birthright Citizenship in the United States: A Global Comparison." Center for Immigration Studies backgrounder, August 2010. http://www.cis.org.

— Preston, Julia. "State Legislators Target Birthright Citizenship with New Laws." *The New York Times*, January 6, 2011. http://www.nytimes.com/2011/01/06/us/06immig.html.

— Vedantum, Shakar. "State Lawmakers Taking Aim at Amendment Granting Birthright Citizenship." *The Washington Post*, January 5, 2011. http://www.washingtonpost.com/wp-dyn/content/article/2011/01/05/AR2011010503134.

— Baker, Bryan C. "Estimates of the Resident Non-Immigrant Population of the United States: 2008." Department of Homeland Security Office of Immigration Statistics, June 2010.

— "Immigration Policy in the United States: An Update." Congressional Budget Office, December 2010.

— Vaughan, Jessica. "Border Crossing Chaos." Center for Immigration Studies blog, March 25, 2009. http://www.cis.org.

— Pew Hispanic Center. "Statistical Portrait of the Foreign-Born Population of the United States 2009." Table 15. February 17, 2011. http://pewhispanic.org/factsheets/factsheet.php?FactsheetID=69.

— "9/11 and Terrorist Travel: Staff Report of the National Commission on Terrorist Attacks on the United States." August 2004.

— North, David. "The 'One-Off' Migrants: A Proposed Fantasy Immigration Policy." Center for Immigration Studies, February 4, 2011. http://www.cis.org.

— E-2 Visas. http://investorvisausa.com.

Chapter 12: Step Five—Love Thy Neighbor

— Morris, Stephen D. "Corruption and Mexican Political Culture." *Journal of the Southwest*, December 22, 2003.

— Caiden, Gerald E. *Where Corruption Lives*. West Hartford: Kumarian Press, 2001.

— Heidenheimer, Arnold J., and Johnston, Michael, eds. *Political Corruption: Concepts and Contexts*. New Brunswick, NJ: Transaction Publishers, 2002.

— Power, Timothy J., and Clark, Mary A. "Does Trust Matter? Interpersonal Trust and Democratic Values in Chile, Costa Rica and Mexico." In *Citizen Views of Democracy in Latin America*. Pittsburgh: University of Pittsburgh Press, 2002.

— Orrenius, Pia, and Zavodny, Madeline. *Beside the Golden Door: Immigration Reform in a New Era of Globalization*. Washington, D.C.: American Enterprise Institute, 2010.

— Sangar, Arti, and Tabja, Federico J. "The Middle East and Latin America: An Investment Partnership on the Rise." DIAZ REUS, 2009.

— Haar, Jerry. "LatAm, Middle East: Expanding Relations." *Latin Business Chronicle*, May 6, 2011. http://www.latinbusinesschronicle.com.

— "Recent and Upcoming Investment." Mexico Business blog, February 9, 2011. http://www.bdp-americas.com.

— Moore, Michael Scott. "Legalizing Pot: Will It End the Mexican Drug Cartels?" *Miller-McCune*, April 6, 2011. http://www.millermccune.com.

— Basmajian, Michael. "Ending the Drug War in Mexico." April 6, 2011. http://www.scribd.com.

— Walker, John. "U.S. Government Helping Arm Mexico in Drug Cartels." March 7, 2011. http://Justsaynow.com.

— Carlsen, Laura. "How Legalizing Marijuana Would Weaken Mexican Drug Cartels." *The Huffington Post*, November 2, 2010.

— Fainaru, Steve, and Booth, William. "Homegrown Pot Threatens Mexican Cartels." *The Washington Post*, October 7, 2009.

— Kilmer, Beau, et al. "Reducing Drug Trafficking Revenues and Violence in Mexico: Would Legalizing Marijuana in California Help?" The Rand Corporation, 2010.

Index